In his extraordinary second collection, Jeffrey Pethybridge confronts the ethical disaster of the torture program that the US used to advance the so-called global war on terror. The poems in *Force Drift* recall Gilles Deleuze's insight that art "is not a matter of reproducing or inventing forms, but of capturing forces." Through the formal range of this dynamic sequence, Pethybridge achieves something like a synthesis of Deleuze's opposition whereby the invention of poetic form becomes the very means of capturing, registering forces: "a reckoning lyric."

The task of reckoning, and rendering visible the violence of the state lies at the heart of the matter precisely because the state intends to conceal, or justify its brutality through the invocation of emergency powers, and the state of exception; or the state disappears persons in its network of black site prisons. Moreover, as the political scientist Darius Rejali has demonstrated, it is in fact democracies that have refined "invisible tortures" such as sensory deprivation, stress-positions, and the waterboard.

Working at the intersection of documentary poetics, and theories of the epic, Pethybridge recommits poetry to a responsibility for a description of history; as a poet-researcher, he asks: "what would be possible...if listening / were the leading-form of being." Driven equally by argument, abstraction, and assemblage, the poems in *Force Drift* address themselves to the irreparable, the "traumaeffect," within the war on terror's record of atrocity. *Force Drift* is cri de coeur, political critique, and essay in the epic.

Against the world-destroying violence of the US torture program, *Force Drift* juxtaposes a catalog of energies, forms, and genres: abolitionist; citational; architectural; chromatic; replete with visual poetries ranging from the arabasques of tzahibs to erasures to extreme measures of leading & kerning. Even when its language is reduced to the pure transcription of pain—aiai aiai aiai—*Force Drift* is committed to aliveness and embodiment as "final treaty of the person," as conscience & counterworld to the history as catastrophe of US imperialism, "irrefutable as the sun to the eye."

"A letter, an essay, an archive, a blueprint, an unredacted CIA file: *Force Drift* exposes what we already know—the 'hell-yellow glare' of American empire escapeless from the glass eye in the sky. Searing in his critique, Pethybridge's anti-epic painstakingly documents & unredacts the machinations of "endless war," disaster capitalism, & the continuous reduction of people into isolated, severed parts forever lost to CIA black sites. The accumulation of *Force Drift* architects the violent patterns of empire—the city, the event, the torture, the missing, the blur between surveillance and black sites. *Force Drift* is an insistent call 'to be new abolitionists.'"

—Andrea Abi-Karam

"Somewhere in the middle of this powerful book, there is an inked hand across the page of a section called passages followed by the line: 'the body tracks in history—'. A powerful summary of the brutally bare remnants Pethybridge is calling up and staying with. Here the alphabet starts with Aleph for Abu Ghraib. *Force Drift* has been some 15 years in the making and it responds forcefully and explosively to the accelerated symbolic and verbal incoherence of our times. Official redaction is here countered as a form of dissident poetics and Pethybridge uses it maximally in his angry, raw and demanding work, which blends landscapes of erasures, dense visual shapes, with exploded, endlessly cyclical, unfinished stories and intercepted thought-processes. A savage, somatised work."

—Caroline Bergvall

Jeffrey Pethybridge is a poet, editor, curator, and sound artist; he is the author of *Striven, The Bright Treatise*. He teaches in the Jack Kerouac School of Disembodied Poetics at Naropa University where he serves as Co-Artistic Director of the Summer Writing Program.

# FORCE DRIFT

# FORCE DRIFT

*an Essay in the Epic*

JEFFREY PETHYBRIDGE

TUPELO PRESS | 2025

*Force Drift: An Essay in the Epic*


ISBN: 978-1-961209-35-0 (deluxe paperback)
ISBN: 978-1-961209-56-5 (trade paperback)
Library of Congress Cataloging-in-Publication Data
Names: Pethybridge, Jeffrey author
Title: Force drift : an essay in the epic / Jeffrey Pethybridge.
Description: First paperback edition. | North Adams, Massachusetts : Tupelo Press, 2025. | Identifiers: LCCN 2025007519 | ISBN 9781961209350 paperback
Subjects: LCSH: Torture--Poetry | Political prisoners--Abuse of--United States--Poetry | Iraq War, 2003-2011--Prisoners and prisons, American--Poetry | Iraq War, 2003-2011--Atrocities--Poetry | LCGFT: Poetry | Essays
Classification: LCC PS3616.E849 F67 2025 | DDC 811.6--dc23/eng/20250409
LC record available at https://lccn.loc.gov/2025007519

Text design by HR Hegnauer Design Studio.
Cover design by Jeffrey Pethybridge with HR Hegnauer Design Studio.

Cover art: Peter Sacks
*Spirit Marker 1*, 2023, mixed media on birch blocks, 120 x 40 x 5 inches
*Spirit Marker 2*, 2023, mixed media on birch blocks, 120 x 50 x 5 1/2 inches
*Spirit Marker 3*, 2023, mixed media on birch blocks, 120 x 30 x 6 inches
*Spirit Marker 4*, 2023, mixed media on birch blocks, 120 x 50 x 7 1/2 inches


First paperback edition August 2025



Tupelo Press
P.O. Box 1767
North Adams, Massachusetts 01247
(413) 664-9611 / Fax: (413) 664-9711
editor@tupelopress.org / www.tupelopress.org

Tupelo Press is an award-winning independent literary press that publishes fine fiction, non-fiction, and poetry in books that are a joy to hold as well as read. Tupelo Press is a registered 501(c)(3) non-profit organization, and we rely on public support to carry out our mission of publishing extraordinary work that may be outside the realm of the large commercial publishers. Financial donations are welcome and are tax deductible.

This project is supported in part by an award from the National Endowment for the Arts.

CONTENTS

## SPECIAL REVIEW

"Poetry, before taking action, listens to the speechlessness of words.

Receiver of the sender who is 'no one.' (As the initial shading out of nothing, the sending of the longest amplitude—the deepest, the slowest—is always a lament.)"

## PAGES 37 TO 43

# Denied in Full

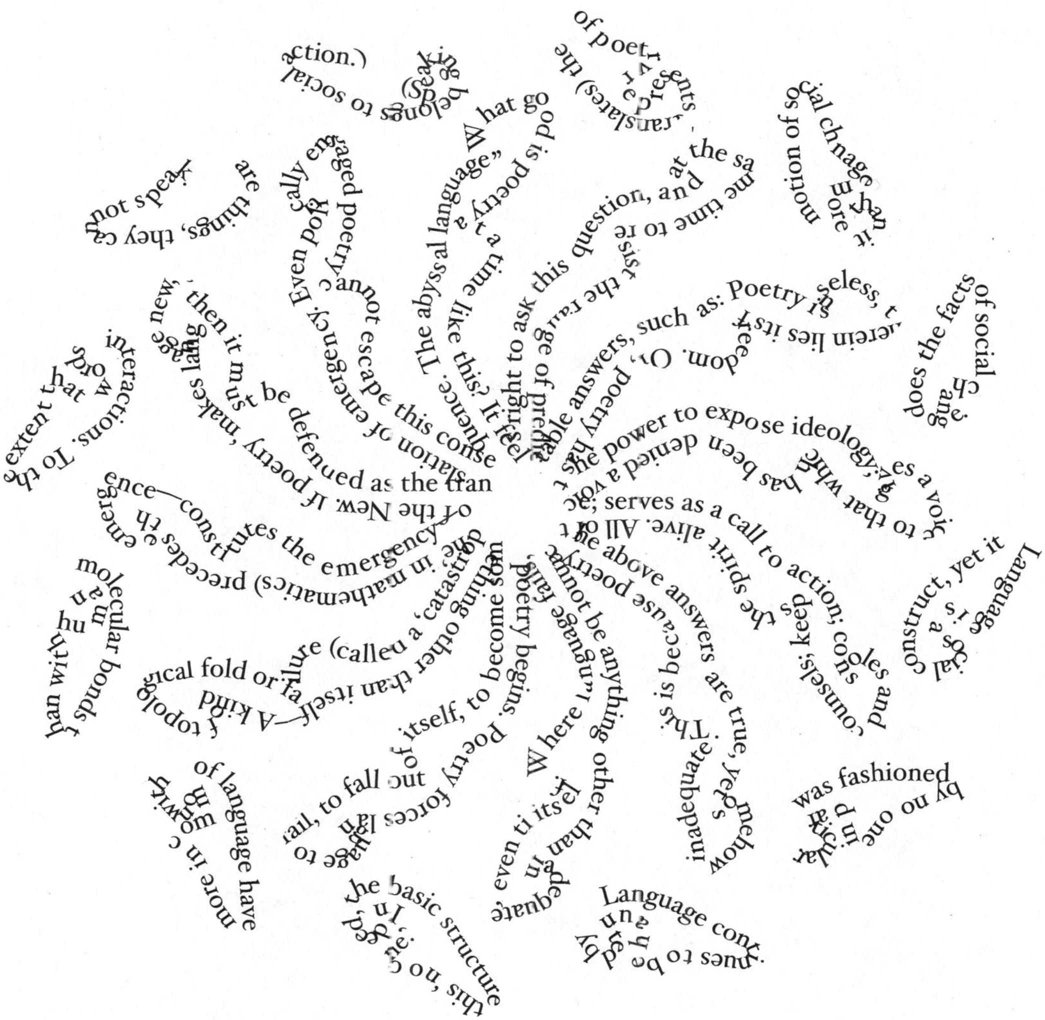

o~~f~~ s~~ay~~ing

system
of
the
~~capa~~city and
its oil ~~capa~~city

of ammunition
city

O, sing, System, of the city and its oil,
city of ammunition, the city
under siege, systematically, being,
Troy at best, a no-fly zone.

under
siege systematically being ~~de=~~
~~s~~troy~~ed~~ at best

a no-fly zone

*Some time during the tenure of the Truth and Reconciliation Commission in South Africa an "unnamed Indian woman" petitioned the Amnesty Committee to grant her amnesty for the crime of "apathy." This anonymous woman's application testified to the moral fact that "individuals can and should be held accountable by history for our lack of necessary action in times of crisis." The application is remarkable in its stripping away the supposed passivity in a "lack of necessary action," for it finds there the criminal act of "exercising apathy rather than commitment." Apathy, her conduct argues, is not a stance devoid of political content, a kind of apolitical ennui; rather, apathy we are told is a political choice over and against "commitment," over and against solidarity with the persecuted; and is therefore, suffused with political meaning, the content of which is nothing less than collaboration, in this case with the apartheid regime of repression, exclusion, torture and administered control.*

*The unnamed woman's confession, and the exacting vision of responsibility and accountability that it implied exceeded the Commission's Mandate, exceeded how the Commission's structuring language understood acts both "whose motivation was political" and that occurred within a bounded period of time (between the Sharpeville Massacre in 1960 and the inauguration of Nelson Mandela as president in 1994). The Amnesty Committee judged the exercise of apathy did "not disclose an action or omission which amounts to an offence or a delict in respect of which amnesty can be granted." The Committee, therefore, denied her application.*

*

(blood-dark, you're floating—the memory
of this story is no utopia,
but a sign along the way, a station
of the crossing, a clearing where she waits,

a clearing, before setting out—
wide, mud-dark river, American night)

Abu Ghraib as the Aleph.

Abu Ghraib as the tragedians would write its sounds: aiai aiai aiai.

A document as irrefutable as the sun to the eye.

A layer of sound, a layer of silence,                sound silence sound inaudible
sound sound sound    silence, a history of pain,

a lever—and spiraling down those vowels.

April now, and what does that mean—new earth is all, and nothing
of world-building spring for Yasser Talal Al-Zahrani,
for Thaar Salman Dawod, for Ameen Sa'eed Al-Sheikh,
for Ali La Pointe, for Rachel, for Joan of Arc.

A prisoner, exhausted—fetal on the floor—in the hell-yellow glare
and greasy light, after his own body was turned into a science
of infliction.

"A 'soul' inhabits him and brings him into existence, which is itself
a factor in the mastery that power exercises over the body.
The soul is the effect and instrument of a political anatomy;
the soul is the prison for the body."

Asymmetrical this warfare, as eyes to the sun, as the will to state-power.

A version of the torture memos in which only aiai, and the names for the many violences remain unredacted.

A version with only the names of the detainees; and could it register as
something other than a memorial, *a demand on future-memory*,
or would you skim it like a catalogue of ships.

A version, as in conceptual art, you make yourself according to three simple
rules;

a whole library of them there in the future city of otherwise & if—
here, now in the small theatre of your reading, a reckoning lyric.

Azaleas outside, April now, red starts in the sun.

~~TOP SECRET~~ as the tragedians would

write its sounds: aiai aiai aiai
aiai aiai

interrogators administered the waterboard to
Al-Nashiri include those vowels

include the 100 names of the lion

**Videotapes of Interrogations**

77. ~~(TS~~ how the man becomes one

how other men become

nothing more decided to
videotape the interrogation sessions.

than cows
to him

include those fighters too
An OGC attorney reviewed the videotapes

78. ~~(TS~~ OIG reviewed the videotapes
in May 2003

their dying physicalities

and history
loud with them

“World, self, and voice are lost, or nearly lost, through the intense pain of torture and through the confession as is wrongly suggested by its connotations of betrayal. The prisoner's confession merely objectifies the fact of their being almost lost, makes their invisible absence, or near absence, visible to the torturers. To assent to words that through thick of agony cohesion to hold its shape as a word of the body enough and none to can be only dimly heard, or to reach aimlessly for the name of a person or a place that has barely of referent, it's a way of sayin, yes, all is almost gone now, there is almost nothing to bond it to its worldly referent, I am making, no longer form my words but the words of another.” left no w, even this voice, the sounds



~~TOP SECRET~~ “The moment of looking is an arrest.”

# Force Drift

*Sometimes a word is a color*—bright apricot, ivory, tortoise gold, *sometimes you are*—
rose smoke, bronze, blue, blue.

"Subject: Eyes Only—Disposition of Magnetic Media ████████████████
████████████████████████████████████████

*Sometimes the world is*—firelight, red, bronze, horn, cold bronze, black, grey, grey,
grey, grey.

"...he does not/not possess undisclosed threat information, or intelligence that
could prevent a terrorist event."

*After the insurrections, I increased security in all aspects of my life.*

"i.e., constant white noise, no talking, everyone in the dark with the guards wearing
a light on their heads...."

*In part this meant a return to communicating in person, and handwritten letters, this is when
I first reached out to you.*

"The best mechanism for destroying the tapes follows."

*The world is full of theories of erasure.*

"████ was so cold that he could barely utter his alias."

*That citation can be a counter-force to redaction, obliteration is the dream of the book.*

"Grown" from a "forest" of nanotubes, Vantablack isn't so much a color, since color is predicated upon reflection.

*Sometimes you are stray light, a stray thought of fugitive hopefulness—sunshine through muslin, pure sapphire.*

And as Vantablack traps 99.965 percent of visible light, it's the virtual annihilation of color.

*Thermal camouflage is listed as a possible military application, which seems almost innocent.*

"Rahman was so cold that he could barely utter his alias."

*I needed the trance, that form of seeing grounded in the epic, the stark brutality of it, to begin to trace the body of the event.*

"Imagine a space that's so dark that as you walk in you lose all sense of where you are, what you are, and especially all sense of time."

*In the forming of the five senses, if that idea of the human remains, if that is a labor of history still.*

"Something happens to your emotional self, and in disorientation one has to reach in for other resources," Kapoor told the BBC.

*This from the future story of our aftermath, the story we will have to write:* "Vantablack grown on all the surfaces of the prison cells essentially rendered them absolute voids."

And then almost at will the sun disappeared.

*And then almost at will the sun disappeared.*

## Note on Method

Of these stanzas, prose and materials, some will need the attack of song; some will crackle along the clouted grain of lo-fi; like staring at the sun, some would blind you if you didn't turn away, others their sun-green blotter afterimages; some show the mock of law within the letter of the law, the law gone intense with lawlessness, as the sponge—intensifies with blood—soaking up the cell's red smear; some will be the documents of this wet-work, albeit redacted to the point of impunity, others under erasure will disclose the truth, the whole truth and nothing but the truth;

some will be set against surveillance, now done in billions and billions of operations, the scale of computations astronomical, algorithm and star-law; some will set the saying of the situation at the lyric/anti-lyric ledge, *since negation may reverse into pleasure, not into affirmation*—and the book must (still) give pleasure, right? Some materials record pain, some chorus it; others the spleen; some will fly the flag of "all right, then, I'll *go* to Hell" (and mean it), others will try and chart the way.

So the constellation through negation, since we're stuck with night.

And because we find ourselves in medias res, out under the field of data-points—like stars; because somewhere in the blank spaces of the data-set, the black-site prisons ghost detainees; because the are facts numbered like stars—like stars—or a catalogue of evidence (for a court that will never come); *because every idea is a sun*, and every sun is a star and every star a sun, because there they are, the falling stars, the fallen suns and numbers, right there on the floor of the Grand Palais—but what good is the sublime, even the sublime halt and rupture now?

So the constellation for navigation: Polaris, Ursa Minor, Southern Cross, star-script (with Mercury in retrograde).

Left with the political imaginary of the book, caught between brackets and barricades, a (new) romanticism—and so what if it is—where critique is protest, and protest vision—vision and star-cant.

## Force Drift

And then almost at will the sun disappeared— / *gold, red, chromium, blue, green, tan, platinum, / sepias*—like a formal rupture, / a volta, like how the inter-title / at the 87 minute-mark of / *In the Mood for Love,* arrives unprecedented, / and out-of-the-blue, cuts into, / and overturns the lovelorn atmospherics / of the film, t h e r e a l arriving / in the form of politics—*platinum, sepias*— / news-footage of de Gaulle arriving / for the transfer of power. And in that clip / the end of French Indochina, / a sign for everything that will come after. Then Chow alone in the ruins—*stone, blue, green, tan*—of Ankor Wat / telling, mouthing his secret into the temple wall....

In the July letter (the letter on betrayal) / she wrote how Wong Kar-wai's film is a sun /in the index of the hope of being / absolutely modern, that beautiful antagonism, precisely for that move, that rupture: / THAT ERA HAS PASSED, NOTHING THAT BELONGED TO IT EXISTS ANYMORE / (you arriving—smuggled in that shipping / container—to your first exile, / and everything that will come after—meaning, / *and then the war came, and nothing was the same.* / Gold. Red. Chromium.

# Force Drift

And then the war came, and nothing was the same,
*gold, red chromium*...the screen night-vision green:

"The war lasted only a few hours; afterwards, everything was different," he says in
the voice-over,

amounting to a philosophy of history,
an image for it there in the burning

oil-fields—*black, red, bronze, gold-black, dark red, gleaming*
*red, yellow-chrome*...
or that cut to Ali La Pointe's eyes,
how radicalization "is VISION,"

in the epic. Once we thought cinema—
the totality of it—was the answer,
once we thought the opposite: "I am

the little drawing," threading—
invisible—this disaster that never sets.

## Force Drift

invisible—this disaster that never sets,
invisible—the body, your body, lost to the ordinary sun,

invisible—the "body as a field of maximum intensity of pain,"
invisible—the swarm of vowels you become therein,

invisible—the 14 distinct cries of pain in *Elektra*, each a knotted
chord of syllables drawn though her human mask and person, which are two

names for the same phenomena, that must appear—we must
appear (to one another) in person, in speech, and in pain, we must

appear in fields of a nowhere state, that first-last paradise
under an ordinary sun, invisible—that classical trace,

invisible—"I come from a country where the bodies were not given back,"
invisible—the "red oxide and black,"

invisible—"his death at DETENTION SITE COBALT,"
invisible—his false testimony on DETENTION SITE GREEN, DETENTION SITE BLUE,

*invisible—the science of torture and infliction as perfected by democracies,*
invisible—*black* [site], *blue, blue, gold, bronze, bronze-wear, blurred-bronze,*

*sunlit-dust, poppy-dotted, glittering...invisible—across a "scarred and*
*lacerated surface," a surface of effects, of power, duress, negation, sudden,*

catastrophic, finding victims everywhere, the end of the sun, lacquer, acrylic,
*"I didn't say this was Realism, but I did want to get at the real."*

## In The Epic

Sing of the new man-of-arms, of all those boy-soldiers fighting like dreaming stoned
on cocaine, hash, or verses, sing of all those boys named 'Kalash,' sing says the epic.

"A victory / over all the gods / under the sun: // the god of love, / the god of debt / with his red-red / avatar, god / c

Everything flows: the Tigris, Irish Road, your thoughts, and the air pungent with cumin lamb...then the explosio
keeping the violence out, become the limits your body breaks against—then the lift-off roar to Ramstein, and ins

And then suddenly the day was a revolution, and the revolution was you, and you were the city,
suddenly, and the city was everywhere, and everywhere teargas, the blinding metastasis of the epic.

"What are you talking about?——you're not making sense.     What victory is out there, just the sea.     Come

At the Ward 57 press conference, the doctor says "I hate to put it this way, but with a sample, a data-set this large
will make radical advances——and very fast." Here they come, the swift blade-footed runners, their metal marath

Playing the airplane, going fast, your hands skim the tops of poppy pods, like you are your own son, then giddy a
you look up and out into the night-vision-green night | "my god, it's full of drones," as many as verses in the epic.

"Father, / you can't under- / stand, you wouldn't / know how to judge // my mind. / It's from my mind / I'll win a m

The long century / the long war argues the animal called history, pacing its cage, wiry and underfed, as its carniva
*The Judge's Injury-Time Psychomacheia & Medicine Show*—drives over the cold-cold, and hallucinatory ground of the

"at the beginning" "when the world was wearied by civil strife" "deranged by violence, intrigue, and finally" "Man
"meanwhile in" "The Annals" "events" "were falsified through terror, and after" "in the praises" "and the hymns c

"Come down from that bridge——you're making me nervous.     Come home, daughter, come and garden—it'll b

In the fable the war is endless: it's waved so long whole eras of fashion have come and gone, and returned again w
One mother rooted her grief into a tree, invasive like the lyric, a spreading chinaberry, and all the war's anthem-b

The hammerlock; the human shield, or firestorm; the red line / green zone incursion; the unconditional
term, your mother tongue; better shock and awe than serve in heaven; the zero sum; so too, the epic.

"I can't tell you, / Father. / My plan // would anger you, / anger any / father."

Soldier-tired: like your own body's some faraway ______*stan*: Jeffreystan, parsley fields
as far as the eye's vigilance....And yeah, Bohemia lies by the sea in the epic.

"The winning of battles is not … ined between men who plan and deliberate, who make a resolution and carry it out, but … which between m … of inert matter,

the little war. // A victory, father, / to suffer their making / no more. Father, // I have no Persia."

and all the walls (the up-armored carrier, flak jacket, your skull)
le your vital signs chirp a counter-measure to the epic's.

home, this year's dogwood is a glory."

cybernetics
n, the march of the epic.

the field's edge

rtyr's / glory."

train—
pic.

*include the superpowers / and their proxies / include the coast of Bohemia / include*
*geopolitics / include the Persian Gulf / include the 100 names of the lion / include th*
*nothing more than cows to him / include the women / and their ululations / the tele*
*you were and set the imaginary loose in you / like unveiled hair /include the fighter*
*overwhelm / the Adversary / include Hector / the idea of Hector / include the hun*
*you / include those fighters, too, says the epic / their dying physicalities / include H*
*how he bears down, tyrannical / laced with all the god-talk / now include the girl*
*apocalypse of unveiled hair and rocket-fire / she has no father, he no daughter / incl*
*least the moral authority of the veteran who guarded the citystate / who came thro*
*of the Future More Vivid / include this world, personed, still / include the lyric less*
*include your own political imaginary, its epic / you must use your voice / like unvei*

executions." "few were left who had seen the republic!" "Thus the State had been revolutionised, and" "and people plunge
the poets" "carried" "through 'the gate of triumph'" "O" "men of Rome" "by your" "soldier" "powers" "into the" "ruining"

the perfect convalescence. Forget the pills; forget the money. (I'm too old for this). Come home, home to our new Pe

th that seductive inflection of the new; human fighters (who grew so few) were replaced by automatons; a new star discove
rds, even the emperor's machine-raptor, binged on the furit, and roosted there in the country of its limbs, stoned, songless,

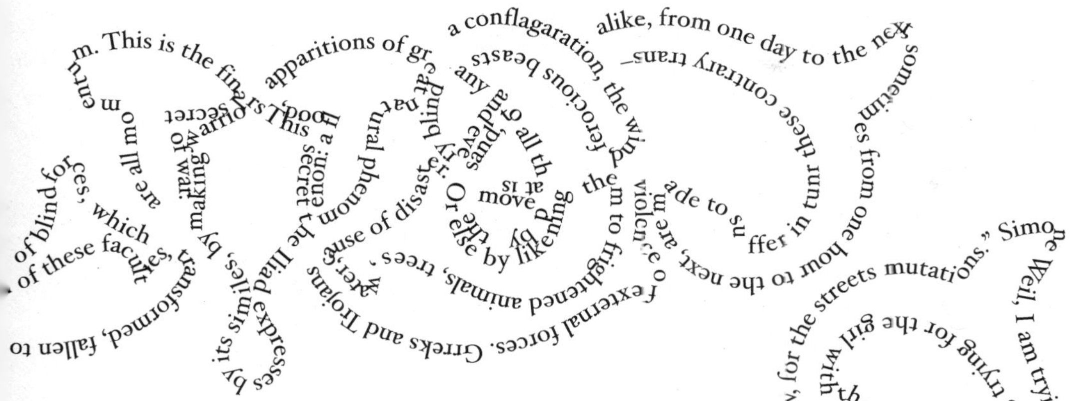


*onomy / its fires / how politics for you was first*
*· / how the man becomes one / how other men become*
*ud with them / how all those vowels torqued the kid*
*strongest birds in your patch of sky / include the*
*e attack / of boys like even thirteen / like you, unlike*
*mphant, now a leader of the Republican Guard /*
*RPG / her revolution, her reckoning / her little*
*ate and love for him / the tether /and if not love at*
*oison gas / include a martyr's glory / include the Shah*
*he anti-epic you're trying for / include the fatwa /*
*nd rocket-fire / reckoned there in the sun of '89*

avery" "to empire"
"and" "spectacle of the" "epic."

f their anthems, and no more epic.

# Force Drift

"I didn't say this was Realism, / but I did want to get at the real," / as in the breaking, irrefutable touch, / insurgent as the lion to the eye, / the eye to the corpse, as the coming realities / of writing endless war, / al-Qa'fāniyy, who breaches the barrier, / lion that collapses walls (any architecture is / a barricade in the discontinuous sky), / that uproots people, sweeps them away, / ethnically cleanses them, as the epic is written— / *tungsten, black, mirror bronze, / sea-green, bronze, red, red, fire-lit bronze*— / "I trust that Simon's intention is to witness something," /

what is poetry for—al-qa'f, verbal noun—/ you demanded of me in your last, / the letter from September, / it's September still or again, / the long century of it, insurgent, / I don't have an answer, obituaries / of friends almost or still daily, / is it just going to be like this, / endless cibachrome, silicone, plexi-glass, / wood frame, 49½ x 60 inches atomized, / swept away in drone hellfire, sudden, catastrophic whir.

and the sum of you
fills that long syllable, because even the person,

Enhanced Techniques

that obsolete rose,
is capable of that, of experiencing
death; or nothing like that, like the absolute
helplessness of locked-in syndrome;

like a mock ex-
ecution; like the water board,
when the new planet is discovered: blue
beyond whatever water meant before,
and you're the chosen astronaut,
lucky, proud, exhilerated by the unique
terror of the undiscovered world—

no, not that, instead, its radical negative:
just the terror, a different kind
of liquid to drown in;
you close your eyes—how could you not—
so sleep (when it comes, when they let you have it)
is rewritten as trauma,
so where in your Book of Dreams, sleep
was the Indian Ocean, you the submarine
underneath its million waves,
invisible,
gliding on your secret mission, sleep now
is suffocating, your skin the million
waves you're under, the million fathoms you
cannot swim back up through,

you wake, because the person, "gold flourisher,"
is capable of that long

## Force Drift

*Impenetrable* | Mona Hatoum
Steel and nylon monofilament
(300 x 300 x 300 cm)
2009

In the sudden
and catastrophic whir

*I propose to consider a dimension of political life*

of the Tate Modern, a cube
composed of empty space

*a dimension of political life that has to do with our exposure to violence*

and 441 barbed-wire
rods suspended in mid-air

*our exposure to violence, and our complicity in it*

arrests and thrills
the mere body you were

*and our complicity in it with our vulnerability*

moving room to room,
now urgent, a revolutionary

*with our vulnerability to loss and the task of mourning*

subject even, a sublime
halt and rupture

*loss, and the task of mourning that follows*

if ever, if ever...
and you yourself aswarm

*that follows, and with finding a basis for community*

with this urgency,
and demand—this vocation—

*with finding a basis for community in these conditions*

in the sudden
and catastrophic world.

## Force Drift

and then
a sudden

and catastrophic
world

you a subtle
body

driven
through

fear
up harsh

walling
driven

under
ego

down harsh
futility

you see
it when

they Mutt
and Jeff

let
seeing in

we know
all

is
power

you mere
body

bare
life

in
isolation
with

threat and
incentive

coffee
a meal

shower
a letter

asylum

*

"touch, too,    is an infinite
system of communication,"  she said,

floating in the pool, and traced an arc
along the light            wave surface   then my arm,

"each living gesture    precarious
which is the root of a latin prayer."

I am Yasser Talal Al-Zahrani, my name is Rachel,
I was discovered at 12:39, they attached wires to my toes,
they say they will rape me, there was a camera there, I am I

did not want my name to be transmitted, I am Joan of Arc,
later they cut out my throat, they catalog my image,
my shame, they archive it, I am proof of the epic.



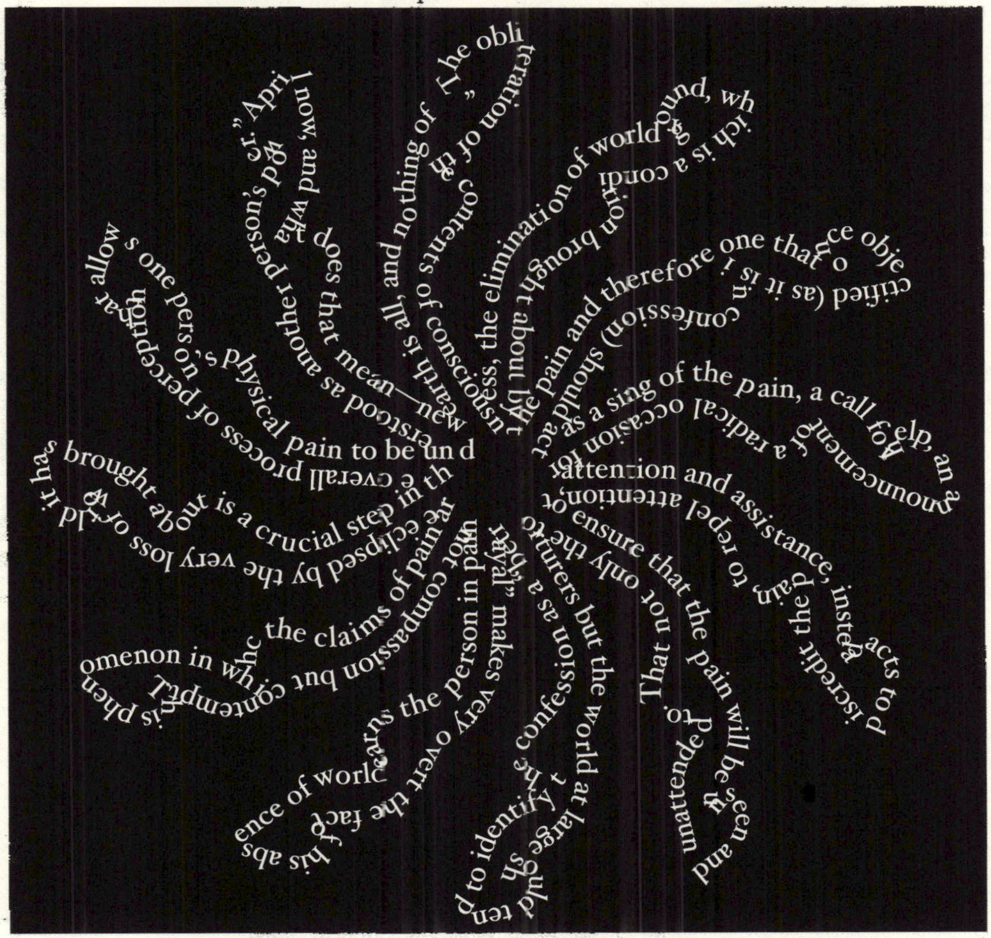

every star is a sun every cell a cage

# Force Drift

"Like how the root of 'precarious'
is a Latin prayer," you wrote that March
the war came, and a few weeks later I recognized the epic

is the world. There is no way around,
only through it—*oyster, lead, blue-grey, gold-*
*grey, blue, translucent…*

                                        if the traumatic event
is both nowhere and everywhere, you
the Lion Whose Prey Is Turned Inside Out,
you the prey;
                              if "for the archive" all fields
are allusive—*brown, green, bronze, blue, blood-red…*

        if into this overwhelm, into this force drift—
without halt,   break,   escape,   or rupture—everything flows:

## Force Drift

If into this overwhelm, into this force drift
        everything, inescapably, flows: *sunset-lit,*
*ember, blue, black, green, redcurrant*...Hiroshima,
        Thebes, Gaza, Saigon, Fallujah, *white* [phosphorous]
*dark wine, gold*..."a phantasmagoria
        of the historical body, and the body-
in-history," being Troy at best a no-fly
        zone—this is what history painting levels out,
blurs into a fire that never sets nor sinks,
        the smears that were towers in *September* reveal
this effacement of politics, this limit——
        it's the painting's genius you showed me, that rainy
August day at MOMA, *ash-streaked, white-water, blue*...
        in the epic all fields are allusive and alight.

# In The Epic

In the field of epic, the classic understanding of Time as *time of war* (eleven score and seventeen...), means time intens
with force—the sponge soaking it up—saturates with its decimations, and their inevitability becomes the meter of th

*Obvious signs of recent battle are general, off to one side the bodies of dead fighters, in the foreground a few small huts or lean-tos occ*

The bomb is capricious: you're alive, and can even hear, but not the guy you were translating for, the stunned dog (wil
everywhere, and all of it reflected there in the oil-black mirror of the security Suburban, like a city in a bottle—an oil-

In the virtual reality of the the underworld, the data-map walls glow white-blue-electric, as the virtually nameless dea
(almost just smoke now) proliferate, while at the podium the unhappy hegemon recounts the 'hard choices' of his epi

ANDROMACHE *comes out of one of the huts carrying her son* ASTYANAX; *as if she is half in this world, and half already els*
*a film montage of images from the war is projected on the skene; the monatge should be highly stylized, inflected with the spirit of cri*

Like a dream of bathers, their liberty and pleasure both, that the image-search just returned, but there is no free
autonomous zone, o men of Athens, no random commons yet secret from the enclosures of the epic.

And suddenly you are your city, and your city is history, and history catastrophe—the Fallujahan women keening
what theorization requires: how, as from a fire that never sinks or sets, would you escape this epic?

*With evident disquiet* TALTHYBIUS *enters followed by a band of* SOLDIERS. *He approaches ANDROMACHE; they exchan*
*seemingly both to* ANDROMACHE *and to himself:* "Look around you, can you see any help or refuge here, anywhere

Fall in the Queen's final square, and the book-bloc bearing shields of citations—a (new) romanticism,
and so what if it is—rush against the cops, against, and out into the riot of the epic.

<< Les femmes sont des machines à souffrir >> thus the falling woman, the grieving mother, the stumbling woman all
as Guernica burns, yet staying upright in *Guernica* << que les machines de résistance, le seules restantes >> see the lan

TALTHYBIUS *bends to tear* ANDROMACHE *from her son, and for a moment he covers her body with his—like a gesture fro*
*The* SOLDIERS *lead her away past the bodies of dead fighters.* TALTHYBIUS, *with evident disquiet, carries* ASTYANAX *b*

In the fable of 1988, squadrons of Iraqi MiGs and Mirages, on 14 separate low-flying sorties, bombarded Halabja with
(blistered, or vomiting, or instantly). One doctor, herself nearly blinded, gathered survivors (stumbling among the cor

That moment, subsuming, into which you and the desert night (star-field) disappear, when the mystic takes out his ow
Then later, after the arrests, and you've done nothing of the kind, as you wander out through the desert of your quara

CASSANDRA *emerges from a hut singing the same mourning song as* ANDROMACHE *before her; she keens with an increasin*

You're fastened to life, this wrong-life, so you have to do something, right, so you go out into the power (blood beatin
what else could you do, you with your romanticism, right Jeff—but then all your similes fail, and you find yourself cau

“The cities too—burned-out Moscow, empty as a deserted beehive Ilion threatened in its opulence, soon to be dethroned and dismembered—ha all their own Holy Troy city

fies
epic.

*pied by the* CAPTIVE WOMEN, *behind them the mostly ruined city-wall; it could be any season.*

-whinning through its deafness), silk-tatters, flames, slick
vorld—which is the epic inside the epic.

Late Letter & Constellation: *Forgive my radic*
*letters, just know that I've been living with the n*
*it's not like I'm the saint's beautiful "to say I love y*
*been reading to one of my neighbors, an old painte*
*why exactly. I was walking by the river down to*
*"4 dead and 2 wounded on Cherokee today. Miser*
*picture of the June clouds. I didn't want to escape*
*thing is now, a way to alloy the base hopelessness–*
*it, I didn't believe it exactly, it was just license to*
*sinking is. You know how deeply I admire both yo*
*science cutting thru all the false analysis masking*
*2001 memo, I found these lines: "To write, finally,*
*less true in war: the cares, concerns / of any final t*
*word / the word it keeps for itself even as it oblite*
*secrecy might also be the non-site (carved out) for*
*dinary flower of the 'I'" Césaire calls it. I've also b*
*I saw some great new scrawls:* sovREIGN pig :
*I added:* fuckthismotherfuckingepic :: poets

*vhere, she sings a mourning song;*
*que, rather than commemoration, ellipitical, and without sound or music.*

*e words mostly inaudible; tonight however, we can hear the messenger say*
*She turns away from him, and falls to a huddle covering her son.*

-heeling under moonlight, lamplight, under the incendiary-blast-light
p-bearer up against the black/white searchlights of the total-war century's epic.

*a dance; the* SOLDIERS *move in, and with some violence separate* TALTHYBIUS *from* ANDROMACHE, *then with greater violence t*
*k toward the ruined city-wall; their images are taken up by the montage, and we see the boy thrown from the wall.*

:hemical agents; the spring air, already greasy from the burnt-oil reek of napalm, turned a satura of sarin, tabun, mustard gas, VX
ses); she tethered them together, and one by one, placed a compress of wet tea leaves on their eyes, and lead them to the evacua

ı heart, weird lantern, and signals by its wet-flickering how you'll make a new politics....
tine—come all the stars down of self-recrimination, those counters, just so many fragments in the epic.

*ntensity then abruptly stops to say:* "Lo, I go to fire." *She walks toward the ruined city-wall, and her image, too, is taken up by the montage; t*

adrenaline-high) of your being becoming your commitments in the book-bloc—
ht between the barricade, and the brackets of the epic.

hey are the geographic religious transfor is accomplished which it was the stake" O sing System, of the city and its oil, city of ammunition, the city under siege, systematically, being The city may be burned to the ground

T where the physical place where the metaphysical crisscross, and the point of gravity. eal centers al lives. They have a soul, a fate, the sacred fic threads of events of faction or man of a stone survives in the epic as a living building but it stands its left the witness to the real or imaginary lives it supported, to the real or legendary struggles of

' can't reckon the reasons for the long span between
'te to you. But what is that?—to say I think of you;
ty I want you to be." Tho I do. I'll write more. I've
one blind, or nearly so, and her doctors can't say
'o smoke, and I got a text from Raphael that read:
nediately after, I held up my phone, and took a
' feeling, maybe just to alloy it. That's all every-
ly said that the other day, but even as I was saying
inking a counter-urgency, an ardency where the
and precision; together they're like a blade, or
ng thru so many excuses. Working with the Sept 16
bsolete rose, / a declaration of 'perfect' secrecy, / is no
he person only." And I know secrecy is the State's
r us: I know I'm data, and that's fine, but a new
heir flowering, invasive like the lyric: "the extraor-
ng again; the other day, smoking behind the library
WRITING / IS / PIGSHIT / ARTAUD
affiti :: *More soon.* *Love J.*

*te* ANDROMACHE *from* ASTYANAX.

drogen cyanide, and thousands died
copters, now refugees of genocide's epic.

*d* *out.*

century's the total-war for Guernica, for Moscow, loud the television liquid sounds, the vowels and prosody of that strange chorus for city burned-out for Troy, for Troy with us now chorus sings with them city on Troy at best, a no-fly zone." O M idea of the Kabul, Kandahar than a war order vision. ded for the a music of Basrah, for Baghdad would you A music breaks through tears, keening w their streets never sinks or sets a fire that from how as acquires in F allusion of this theorization theorization that all those loud with what the wall's how the vowels battle are general: cities are Aleppo to Zagreb, from graffiti their dying physicalities. Of the future cities, some will crackle along the clouted graffiti the song, some will need the attack of song, that is written on their obvious signs of recent

# Force Drift

*In the epic all fields are allusive and alight*:

under the algorithms of surveillance, gone
is the innocence from the the two-word poem search engine,
a rhyme with siege-engine now.
                                                  (A mural crown
was the Roman trophy for the soldier who over-
took the enemy-city's wall).
                                        Light palm-shadows here,
in the hours writing you this morning I remembered
that photo from the early June internet—the siege
of Kobanê defeated—of the woman standing tall
in the back of the pick-up, desert horizon behind her,
taking off the all-black disguise she needed to cross
ISIS-controlled territory, revealing her magnificent
red dress, yellow and turquoise solar swirls—a perfect
image to end a film, | or history——the message you sent:
"to wear a beautiful dress is a human right."

## Force Drift

To wear a beautiful dress
is a human right

(and no less true in war);
to look up into a clear

day-sky, and not fear
a signature strike; to walk

through your city, no
curfew, no checkpoints;

to be utopian—even
if only for the duration

of the ~~poem~~ thought; to swim
in the sea (and in thought)—

all human rights,
o extraordinary flower

of the "I," to meet you
in that secrecy,

there in the folds
of that obsolete rose,

that universal
treaty of the person,

find me so that I might
exist—we might

exist in that human
right, the anti-epic

we're trying for—
*blue-black, black water, sky-blue,*

*redquartz, background dark*—
I'm always writing you.

# Force Drift

*Redquartz, background dark*—I'm always writing you in rückenfigur, you, the
guide, out ahead leading the way through—*overlight, tidal light*—

into the violent abstract of the disaster, how it burns our time-sensitive skin:
"Look," you say, "the person, the idea of it, is running out, can you see it, look—

'Blake's eyes'—there in the sheltering, obscure, a trace of graffiti in the ruins of
what we persist in calling the world"—*gold, silver, red, indigo-skinned*—

"To ask for recognition, or to offer it, is precisely not to ask for recognition for
what one already is. It is to solicit a becoming, to instigate transformation,
to petition the future always in relation to the Other," Butler writes.

And yet sometimes the man becomes a lion, The [One Who Equals] Ten, how
other men are nothing more than cows then corpses to him, The Ten, Whose
Voice Grows Louder With His Victims.

"Who counts as human? Whose lives count as lives? And finally, What makes
for a *grievable* life?"—that first-last right of the human,

the feeling without which—into the earth—without which your sister's hands,
your mother's hands search for your body—

disappeared or wasted in the open air—for it was their hands your body to sew,
their voices, shroud of vowels, to bury you

(outside, the grass still wet from it all) in the epic—*red, bronze, lime-scoured-bronze*—
The force of your plea, its vision and renunciatory ethic, the sublime halt

and rupture of it, is: we know the answers, know whose lives are reckoned as
human, and we know why; the task is to overturn those answers, to be new
abolitionists.

(What am I to you: pilgrim, lover, ally, archivist, foreign correspondent, nearest
thought?)—*tungsten, dark grey, daylight*—"irreparable

as Apollo," the laws and vows issued from the Research and Fatwa Department,
issued from the Secretary of Atrocities, issued from the wounded Sphinx
(as he paces

the cinema-room). I know you've been despairing, don't, we need you, your
mind (ardent, precise) is the magic sword to light this descent—*malicious
lazuli, frosted iron, far black*—

forgive my silences [                    ], my lost commitments therein,
I'll write more. I love you; I want you to be. | "I'll be your mirror," I'll be
your Imaginary.

to write

Finally that

obsolete rose

a declaration of

"perfect"

secrecy

To write, finally, of that obsolete rose,
a declaration of "perfect" secrecy,
is no less true in war. The cares, concerns
of any final treaty of the person only—

is no less true in war the cares concerns

of

any final treaty

*of the*

person only

# Force Drift

I'll be your mirror, the book your Imaginary
        in the aftermath, in the fields of that future
less vivid where human action will be yet alive

        to becoming the kind of revolutionary grace
we're trying for, contra epic, contra the hell-yellow
        searing—the dogs are barking now, the dogs a pack

of maximum of decibels—of the body's openness
        to sound turned into a science of infliction (months of it,
that long manufactured night, the sentence) and the deeper

        this descent takes us—*gold, gold, silver, sea-dark, bronze,*
*all warwear pearl*—It's not "The Dying Gaul" inside
        their barking, it's a rack, "a phantasmagoria [of sound]

of the historical body, [all war-loud-torn, loudest pitch
        ever, and the cities, bodies gone therein] and the body-in-history,"
your body (o vessel of the "I") through which The Overwhelm,

        The Lion Who Multiplies Until All Else Is
Eclipsed eclipses you, or swallows you,
        or in the brutal fact of the prison torture room you

become nothing but absolute vulnerability—
        "ragged" the poem wanted to say, but it's total
this annulment of your human person,
                                        the Sphinx's meaning, its mark.

# Force Drift

"ragged" the poem wanted to say, but it's total, The Overwhelm, this annulment
of the human person, gone loud, the brutal fact of the prison torture room—a louder violent
even when its gone—The Lion Who Multiplies Until All Else Is Eclipsed eclipses you,
and precisely by will the sun disappears into this force drift, excruciatingly, it swallows you,
the Sphinx's meaning, your absolute vulnerability—*redcurrant-colored, white-leopard,*
*white, red-sepal, fierce-chrome, weapon-grade chrome*...unto the Capitol, enthroned,
the glare of a thousand emergency powers—*silverwool, gold, gold, bright red, mirror bronze*...
down through the gates:

DEPARTMENT OF TOTAL INFORMATION, DEPARTMENT OF BLOOD AGENTS, CENTER FOR INTENSIFICATION STUDIES, THE SWARM PROGRAM, CRISIS INSTALLATION AUTHORITY, DEPARTMENT OF SENSATION AND OBLITERATION—its "blue-lit stage," loud, brutal, and I know the call for a court is the enemy, I know the call for a court is still the enemy.

# Ab lish

abolish something starting with the schoolchy, the folds of a beautiful

of the person, that final treat treatise on perfect secre

that final treat, we were trying for, that

say, gold red, chromium, of anti-epic w classical trace, I heard you

americas, abolish the cinema—I mm, its blue-lit theatr e of pain, abolish says every wall in this city, because we painted it there in the insurrentionary

resifications of desire for nothing that was a remnant of the last regime, pure value-form of capital, gold, red, chromium I heard you say of our bodies

crisis in the sudden, violent punctuations of becoming our commitments in the square, and hereafter under the abolitionist sun, everything flows, strange

flora from the flashback, feral bw gleaming, red, yellow-chrome, mirror-black, the leading form of attack against the security-state, monstrous sphinx swarming all the way to the end of your beautiful death, abolish how for certain

And then almost at will the sun disappeared
then almost at will the sun disappeared
almost at will the sun disappeared
at will the sun disappeared
will the sun disappeared
the sun disappeared
sun disappeared
disappeared
appeared
pear
red

# Book X an essay in emergent night

*So we begin at night*

Like beginning with the statement of argument, a decalogue—

1.0: That the disaster seen clear through to   is an impossibility,
1.01: and writing towards it, a kind of militancy.

[illegible]

2.0 Century & sentence;  dirt, and syllable; *gold, mirror-bronze*—
"and the subject's sensuous contact brought to a driving
& minimal condition, a crisis of ________"; animal; night; film—
among the several seven forms of time weaponized in the epic.

"The use by CIA of the following techniques"

"The use by CIA"

1.1: The disaster seen (clear)
through thick paint, dirt-glint—
*silver-black*— tar, straw, lead,   gold—
*gold, black, bronze, weapon-grade chrome*:
a debris-field;  so too, the epic;

"the following
techniques"

Centuries are seas
centuries
are salvages

you wrote
from exile

fugitive
worlding
elsewhere

as which
must bear

"boil and life"

coffee
a meal
shower

a letter
asylum

—using the same
password
same route

[illegible]

3.0: That emergent night is a state of exception,
3.0.1: that this is both real night (close to you now)
3.0.2: and a necropolitical zone.

1.1.1: so too, the anti-epic we're trying for—

1.1.1.1: as in the the film-clip—the timbre of it—
of Darwish saying (in the subtitles): "I'm looking
for the poet of Troy....I wanted to speak
in the name of the absentee...."

d, yellow-chrome, bronze, gold-black, fire-lit, bronze,—of the underlying mechanisms of how I am in the
[illegible]
ld you say of or through metastasis [evidence of battle is sharp, and general (large fragments of blasted city

*So we begin at night [and state of emergency] already two watches old,*
*so you have to hurry thru the thigh-tall rushes,*
*you have to hurry in your terror-armor*——

"constant
white-
noise"

" no
talking"

"By the end of December 2002, the CIA Renditions Group that had visited DETENTION SITE COBALT had concluded that the detention facility's initial 'baseline conditions' involved so much [sensory] deprivation that any further deprivation would have limited impact on the interrogations."

4.0: "A word is a no-place for the encounter to take place,"
4.0.1: that we held this between us as a credo,

4.0.2: a perfect secrecy (ephemeral, autonomous)—
4.0.3: a cypher / for the (open) city; listening for it ~~in the epic~~.

*You have to hurry*
*out under the murky night*
*already two watches old,*
*toward the enemy line.*

"everyone in the dark with the guards wearing a light on their heads when they collected and escorted a detainee to an interrogation cell, detainees constantly being shackled to the wall or floor, and the starkness of each cell (concrete and bars)."

*glad when you hear the heron's cry,*
*glad at hearing Odysseus of all the answers—*
*who recognized the omen—*
*pray to his patron:*

"Hear me, Athena,
you who have allied my every work,
you who have tracked my every move
in your brilliant surveillance,
show your absolute love of me again:

let us walk back to our ships,
and to kleos—*gold, red, chromium, bronze*—
the long centuries of it, for this raid
that will devastate the Trojans."

3.1: That the tenth book of the *Iliad*,
a book of ambush, of beheading, a book of chiastic
structure (also called epic regression)
occurs precisely in this zone
of necropolitical, emergent night.

3.1.1: What is it / that it is also close to you now?

3.1.2: What is it / that because it is the book
in which he's murdered, it is called the Doloneia
not as elegy, or critique—just simple convention,
indexical, of the epic.

5.0: The problem of force is in its devastations.
5.0.1: Some theories call this law the world.
5.0.1.1: The world is lawless epic is the lion.

*And you prayed too, citing your father's victory*—red,
red, weapon-grade bronze—*citing*

*also the heifer, with gold-plated horns, you'd sacrifice*
*if you survived this night-mission*—

Pallas Athene heard their prayers,
and unlike some nights said yes.
And they set-out like two panthers
under the black night

and through the thigh-tall rushes—
still wet from the day-long slaughter—
through the corpses, the armor,
and the black blood.

And in the Trojan camp
one fighter, Dolon, volunteered
for night reconnaissance,
and set-out through emergent night
over that same plain of dark earth.

5.1: The problem of force lies in the traumaeffect

“complete”

“darkness”

“including visions, paranoia, insomnia, and attempts at self-harm”

5.1.1: that everynowhere driving assault,
disintegration you’re thrown against & under—

“constant”

[illegible]

*gold, gold, red-earth, mirror-bronze, weapon-grade bronze*—being a body & person in the epic.

“white-noise”

*—black-bronze,*
*dark red,*
*dirt-glint—*

A fighter crossed over that same plain of black earth.

*And you heard him out in the night—*
*just as Odyssesus was saying:*

“counter-terrorism”

“Diomedes, someone is coming from their camp.
I can’t tell if he’s out to spy on us in our ships,
or if he’s just out to loot the many the corpses.
Wait, let him pass by; and then we can seize him from behind;
don’t let him outrun us; don’t let him escape;
keep him hemmed in with your spear—drive him
away from their camp and towards our ships;
don’t let him back to the shelter of the city.”

When we arrived
at the safehouse in ______

it was the anniversary
of the twentieth revolution

we went to a small underground
ceremony, it was snowing

[illegible]

on the beach; I dreamt again
of Zanzibar: pigeons

the sounds of boys, his hands
moving into the columbarium

indefinite, posthuman there
a ghost detainee, you wrote,

but weirdly can’t hold
the time of it in mind:

night or mirror-bronze day;
sometimes I feel his name

is Kalash, or Suleiman,
other times no one dying

indefinitely sentenced
to emergent night

3.2: That emergent
night is a state of

exception, is invisible,
or ‘at the threshold

of detectability,’
eliding  pixel by pixel

into deniablity,
impunity, beyond

any resolution
of the satellite

image (fractaling
tazhib)—*background*

*blue*, *black-bronze, gold,*

*fire red, wet red, dirt-*
*glint*—(witness

nothing) the lion,
invisible, cruising

its drone-ruined
kingdom / hunt

in the epic.

*Odysseus of all the answers*
*said this half in speech,*
*half in tactical sign language,*
*which in its way foretold the future*
*of the Trojan more clearly than even a seer’s prophecy.*

*Odyssesus lay*
*chest pressed*
*to the cool earth,*

*and his hand*
*showed halt,*
*then went flat,*

*then shot back*
*—moonlit—*
*a half-fist,*

*thumb pointing over his shoulder,*
*then flashing open, his hand became a grabbing fist*

*then opened to show the empty palm,*
*and turned to swipe the nothing there away,*

*and then spread all its fingers like a fork jabbing the air,*
*and finally his hand turned into a fist,*

*and you could see your prisoner rendered there—*

remember, you
wrote, losing time

and effacement
of bare contact

with the sensuous
fact of the world

*brutally enforced*

corrode & annul
the final treaty

of the person;

even just those
minimal seasons

of being  in hiding
stripped me down

broke my  mind
chemically,

[illegible]

So they hid there among the corpses,
waiting for their future prisoner.

"c o n s t a n t
w h i t e - n o i s e"

the way both
the cancer

& the cancer drugs

left me
a double ghost

And elsewhere Dolon quit weighing the danger of the night-mission
versus Achilles' magnificent horses & chariot—so intricately inlaid with bronze

that even sitting still the metal flows like a tangle of snakes in the glare of sunlight—
which was to be his prize, Dolon stole thru the plain and into the trap [of the epic].

*Then you two captains took off after him.*

When he heard them coming, he hoped
that the noise was his friends coming
to tell him to abort the mission,
since Hector had ordered the army to withdraw,

and he could forget the image of that writhing,
glistening metal. But when they closed
to a spear's-throw-length, Dolon knew
they were enemies—and he ran.

*—black-bronze, dark red, star-glint—*

"visibly shaken by his hallucinations depicting dogs mauling and killing his sons and family."

"c o u n t e r -
t e r r o r i s m"

*And as he ran, you and Odysseus chased him,*

*you chased him, your heart swollen*
*with adrenaline & discipline*
*like a dog released into the rush of the hunt—*

*all your master made you for*
*just out there in the night,*
*out there for you to bring it down—*

5.2: The problem of force is in its disposessions—

5.2.1: in the impossibility of possessing its violent epiphnay,

*Do you hear that Diomedes?*
*Do you hear your own name*
*in the echo of your combat*

*pulse. Can you hear it*
*through the white noise*
*of the future less vivid?*

5.2.2: and the terrible delusion that one could possess it,

*Like two sharp-fanged dogs trained to hunt:*
*you pressed after him like he was a doe*
*or rabbit—and because this night*

*the poem was yours—he was*
*just such quarry, such little prey*
*for you, and Odysseus sacker of cities*

5.2.3: when one is nothing than mere conduit—

[illegible]

5.2.4: quicksilver writ(h)ing—*gold-black, mirror-bronze, dirt-glint*—

*And just before he reached sentries guarding*
*the fast ships, Athene put a force inside*
*you so that no other fighter among*

5.2.5: devoid of logic, order, mercy—“pitiless” Simone Weil calls

*the bronze-armored Achaeans could claim*
*this collar, this kill. And so you shouted*
*in your war-cry voice:*

*“Stop, or I’ll catch you with my spear,*
*and I promise, you will not long escape*
*your sheer destruction at my hand.”*

5.2.6: the economy of violence & temporary ‘victory’ in the epic

The spear’s bronze point, first a polished
streak out of the corner of Dolon’s eye
then a nail, as it sailed
just over over his shoulder,
to punctuate the threat.

5.2.7: “hateful cycle” Mbembe calls the lawless law wherein victim

Like a goofy cartoon
is how you saw him
seized by terror,
his face drained of living color
from the fact of his death,
proximate—*mirror-bronze, black-bonze, dark*

5.2.8: now exectuioner later—*sun-loud, dirt-glint, blood red*—is the epic.

4.1: The no-place
of the lyric / the no-

place of the world in
which we can never

meet—*glassy, black-*
*red, dirt-glint, fire-red,*

*dark earth, bronze,*
*bronze, wet-red,*

*bronze*—beyond dis-
aster, driven (red

flare) to the ground-
form of the enemy

(smoke billowing
through the avenues,

in months the city is
ruins) wherein white

terror constant force
(do you hear that

quiet) is emnity as pure
realtion is the epic.

*—out there in the thigh-tall rushes,*
*out there in your terror-armor,*

*out under the aparthied*
*of emergent night, you almost laughed*

*at you enemy, now prisoner*
*or corpse, depending on your will,*

*but that sound*—gold, black, mirror-
bronze—*biting at your hearing,*

*that sound—your own 'beautiful death'*
*high-whinning toward a limit-*

*pitch like an engine (martyr-*
*heart) you're burninmg up*—gold-black,

red earth, wet red, fiery red,
weapon-grade bronze—*for the epic*

| "constant" | "constant | white-<br>noise" |
|---|---|---|
| "counter"<br>"noise" | | "white"<br>"terror" |

"completedarkness"
"completedarkness"
"completedarkness"
"completedarkness"
"completedarkness"
"completedarkness"
"completedarkness"

only a disremebering

between us as if two
echo a response,

you wrote: I read
a research finding

once where several
people in the study

were intensely more
open to the effects
of hypnosios;

virtuosos,
the psychologists
called those who could

enter the delusion
so completely that they
refused to recognize

themselves in video
footage being inter-

viewed—I felt like that
utterly estranged from

my image & thinking

[illegible]

“including
visions
paranoia
insomnia
andattempts
atself-harm”
“waskeptin
totaldarkness”
“fortwoandahalf
yearsheremained
insocial
isolation”
“constant
noise”
“completedarkness”
“constant””white
“terror”
“counter”
“visions”
“including”
“complete””terror””
“including”
“antipsychotic”
“darkness”
“totaldarkness”

"Take me prisoner,"
he said already crying

"left in his cell"

"approximately six weeks"

"subjected to eight extensive sleep depirvation sessions"

"longest a total of 138.5 hours"

"shackeled in a standing position"

2.1: Time in the body / the body in time is both an excruciating circuit of pain, and bare rhythmic-ground (measure) of being in the epic.

2.1.1: Time then is
black earth—bodies
going into it; time

is apparatus: pure
capture of the living,
their many gestures,

ideas, desires, dis-
courses among days
& architectures &

the thigh-tall grasses—
still-wet with it all;
time is subjegation

to force / to force and
its decimations; time,
therefore, is empire:

always & everywhere
a limit—impossibility—
(you feel it sill, here

in this no-place)
of escape, or over-
throwing immortal epic.

"Take me prisoner," he said almost to no one there—
no one, or emergent night, "take me prisoner"

" c o n s t a n t w h i t e - n o i s e "
" c o m p l e t e d a r k n e s s "
" c o n s t a n t " " t e r r o r "
" 1 3 8 . 5 h o u r s "
" v i s i o n s " " p a r a n o i a "
l i k e " a n y s p e c u l a t i v e l a n g u a g e "
" w a s k e p t i n
t o t a l d a r k n e s s "
" f o r t w o a n d a h a l f
y e a r s h e r e m a i n e d
i n s o c i a l
i s o l a t i o n "
" c o n s t a n t "
" n o i s e "
" c o m p l e t e d a r k n e s s "
" c o n s t a n t " " d e p r i v a t i o n "
" i n h i s c e l l "

"and I will ransom myself, my father will pay you
any price; back home we have bronze, mirror-bronze,
Arabian horses, and gold, & worked-iron,

and more gold still—my father will pay you
anything if he just hears that I'm alive,
a prisoner among the hollow ships. Please."

those years lost

(tho somehow tightly
framed) return in nights

of sleeplessness
of self-recrimination

those nights in which
each memory (if they

can be called that)
is a token of survivor's
guilt even when what

survives is less person
than combine
of tendencies, the same

password, the same
locality for a season

of relent of aslyum

coffee a meal shower

a letter to you—

6.0: How, Kristeva asks, can the truth of pain be spoken,

when the available rhetorics of literature,    and even everyday speech

somehow always seem    festive?

6.0.1: Only by subverting this festive rhetoric, she writes—by distorting it,

by rendering it awkward, clumsy, broken, strained,    making it grate—
abstracted, intense, abject, monstrous—

6.0.2: only then might the censoring blank of pain itself be overcome, flickering—

*fire-lit red, gold, gold, mirror-bronze*—through & against emergent night.

d, an emergent kind, albeit lesser, this new lividity, undead, I am I did not want to be detained among the carcinogens, and

6.1: Whispered on the line,
whispered, urgently,
from the twentieth century
archive—a brutal snowy
April—*grey, grey, rose smoke,*
*white leopard*—
comes the question:
"can you describe this?"

" D e n i e d i n f u l l "
" D e n i e d i n f u l l "
" D e n i e d i n f u l l "
" D e n i e d i n f u l l "
" D e n i e d i n f u l l "
" D e n i e d i n f u l l "
" D e n i e d i n f u l l "
" D e n i e d i n f u l l "
" D e n i e d i n f u l l "

Then Odysseus
with all the answers said:
"If we wanted you dead,
you'd be dead already,
Trojan; beilieve me, ransom
is worth more than your corpse,
this war dragging on a decade;
tell us what you're after
here in the swift-dark night"

" D e n i e d i n f u l l "
" D e n i e d i n f u l l "
" D e n i e d i n f u l l "
" D e n i e d i n f u l l "
" D e n i e d i n f u l l "
" D e n i e d i n f u l l "
" D e n i e d i n f u l l "
" D e n i e d i n f u l l "
" D e n i e d i n f u l l "

6.1.1: 'this' being the disaster—
being enfolded within force,
within the overwhelm &
aporia of the traumaeffect—
'this' being the stripping away
of all—*wet-red, dirt-black,*
*tungsten, red-dark*—of all
human senses but infliction.

feels like that constant white noise, naked, enforced, corrosive ... of the person, strange flora in the flashback. "The shit is

“deprivationoflight
andauditoriystimuli”
“threatandincentive”
“egodownharsh”
“total
darkness”
“emotionalhate”
“fearupharsh”
“weknowall”
“constantwhite-noise”
“futility”
“stresspositions”
“constantwhite-noise”
“including
“thewaterboard”
“visions
paranoia”
“silence”
“complete
“silence”
“completedarkness”
“emotional
love”
“establishyouridentity”
“fearupmild”
“constant”“terror”
“repetitionapproach”
“hooding”
“complete”
“hallucinations”
“antipsychotic”
“darkness”
“mockburial”
“black-site”
“white”“terror”

6.1.2: 'this' being beyond all technologies of description,
we sought instead a way to register,   to capture forces—
like photosensitive paper, an array of facts
under the irreperable sun—*gold, gold, gold fire-lit bronze*—
the sun as total infomation awareness,      eye of the epic.

cinogenic dust—pink teeth, a sigh in the mouth, me and the wasps paper makers, the other dead won't touch the st

| | |
|---|---|
| | 3.3: That emergent night is a matrix of weponized decibles: |
| "Are you out here among the corpses looking for a trophy, to strip one for its armor;<br><br>or did Hector order your reconnaissance—to search out all that goes on in our camp,<br><br>and the hollow ships; or was this night-mission your own idea; tell us now." | 3.3.1: as in BODIES turned up louder than the pain threshold,<br><br>or the endless loop & environment of FUCK YOUR GOD;<br><br>3.3.2: as in the torturer's voice pressed to its own limit yelling<br><br>in a proximity that should only be the lover's or mother's |
| | 3.3.2.1: and at that point blank proximity it's no longer a human |
| "What an empty dream Hector built in me:<br><br>'like quicksilver seething as if it were a living thing; like a tangle of mambas writhing—*oil-black, black-bronze, mirror-black, gold, star-glint;* like even the high irreperable sun shattered over sea-waves—*fire-lit bronze, gold, weapon-grade chrome*—even sitting still—imagine it Dolon—the bronze-work of Achilles' chariot moves & hums, and will be your prize for this night-mission.'" | voice (for summoning), but an instrument for inflicting pain,<br><br>a chimera of the State & man: the vicitm's own scream (100db)<br><br>a feedback loop to drown in—<br><br>3.3.3: as in that everynowhere "horrible ghost laughter," acousmatic, |
| | meaning: *you are in a place that is out of the world;* |
| | 3.3.4: and you cannot shut your hearing down, cannot stop it— |

o be the long century of it, the school of the Aleph, bare life, digital, sexual humiliation, naked, "constant white noise, no talkin

you say of or through metastasis [evidence of battle is sharp, and general (large fragments of blasted city s

cannot stop your skin, your nerves, cannot close this openness

D e t e n t i o n S i t e G r e e n T h a i l a n d

to the air, cacophonous, brutal with energy—*black, black, gold-black,*

D e t e n t i o n S i t e C o b a l t A f g h a n i s t a n

*wet-red, fire-lit bronze*—that envelops you in excruciaitng sound-time:

D e t e n t i o n S i t e B l u e P o l a n d

"global war on terror" "emergent night" "immortal epic."

and for all that, it was just
hearing your voice

(after the years across waves,
the years of radio silence)

albeit digitally in the voice-
over of the Mural communique,

the glimpse of your hands,
writing, moving over the glassy
surface of the possible:

like the idea of escape,

the refusal of any timeframe
genetic to this long century
of cruel modenrity;

like this speculative
& broken anatomy

like wind moving

through your hair, scarf,
in desert-light, a garment

in an almost living gesture—
the video-clip ends like that

7:0 That emergent night is a burning screen of lawfare—

7.0.1: is the lawlessness of the state of exception
through which both the State, and law itself enter into history,

D e t e n t i o n S i t e G r a y A f g h a n i s t a n t

7.0.1.1: and history—itself a burning screen—*gold, red, chrmoium*——
and which might more truly be called *wartime.*

D e t e n t i o n S i t e B l a c k R o m a n i a
D e t e n t i o n S i t e I n d i g o G u a n t a n a m o B a y
D e t e n t i o n S i t e M a r o o n G u a n t a n m o B a y
D e t e n t i o n S i t e O r a n g e A f g h a n i s t a n

7.1: "the music program" " the disposition matrix" "the cinema-room"
"the disco" "Enhanced Interrogation Techniques" "a signture strike"
all sites & programs of lawless law within the "operational history" of the epic.

D e t e n t i o n S i t e V i o l e t L i t h u a n i a
D e t e n t i o n S i t e B r o w n A f g h a n i s t a n

“aftertheplaceof
darkness
wastheplaceof
sterile,white
light
Herethey
blazedlight
thatwas
brightandintense

becauseofthe
sterile
white
ofthewalls,
floorsandceilings.
Hereit
feltasif
Iwasliving
inarefrigerator”

“Theytoreoff
allcfmyclothing.
Oneshoved
afingerintomyrectum.
Theyphotographed
menaked.
Thentheyput
adiaperonme
andpluggedmyears

withcotton,
placedheadphones
andahood
overmyhead,
andsecurely
tapedthehood.
Theychained
myhands,waist,andfeet.
Iwasblind,deaf.”

“Istill
suffer
theexcruciating
physical
andmental
effects
ofmytime
inthe
Darkness“

ze, gold-black fire-lit bronze—of the underlying mechanisms of how I am in the e

“Subjectbegantocry
andpleadedagainhisdenials”

swarming with the casualties, of or through metastas

“Emptier still was Hector’s dream for you,
since only immortals, or those fighters
proximate to immortality—*gold,*

*red, chromoium, weapon-grade bronze*—can drive
Achilles’ chariot, and you’re nowhere
close to immortaliy are you, boy?”

“ t h r e a t a n d i n c e n t i v e ”
“ w e k n o w a l l ”
“ f u t i l i t y ”
“ s i m u l a t e d d e a t h ”
“ t h e w a t e r b o r a r d ”
“ c o m p l e t e d a r k n e s s ’
c o n s t a n t w h i t e - n o i s e ”
“ c o n s t a n t ”
“ w h i t e ” “ t e r r o r ”

Odyssesus of all the answers said
with terrible sincerity, and started
the interrogation: “where is Hector now?

where his horses & armaments?
what are his plans? will they return to the city
after this victory? & who keeps the watch?”

“ s u b j e c t
w a s t h e n t o l d
t o g e t i n t o
t h e s m a l l b o x ”
“ t h e b e s t
m e c h a n i s m
f o r d e s t r o y i n g
t h e t a p e s ”
“ t h e f o l l o w i n g t e c h n i q u e s ”

ed, dry submarine, dirt submarine, swarming with the casualties, of or through metastasis, and the underlying phenomenon is still a

"Theyusedthis musictotortureus. Itwasblastingallaround. Therewerespeakersin everycell. Therewashardlyanyway tosleep. Itwas likeaperpetualnightmare... itwasmeanttodriveyounuts"

6.2: That pain is an "incontestable reality,"

"Mywhole body stillaches, myupperand lowerbackespecially. Iregularly suffercrippling flashbacks

6.2.1: and the pure force of its incontestability reflects back

andnightmares. They'rea constantreminder ofthatplace andtheterrible things thatweredonetome there."

on the one with the questions, "world-destroying" sphinx

there"inhiscell" "blackedout"there"in theconditioningroom" hiddenthereamongthe"redactions" therein"thedisco" therein"cagessupplied byalocalcontractor"

there between the walling wall, and the waterboard.

There in emergent night,     and being
so far from immortality—
Donlon answered them with clear,
and actionable intelligence,
[which is the lie of torture's epic].

“rape”

“mockexecution”

“constant”

“white”“terror”

“deprivation

oflight

andauditoriy

stimuli”

“hooding”

“total”

“hallucinations”

“antipsychotic”

“darkness”

“constant”

“emotionalhate”

“complete”

“suicidal”

“darkness”

“electro-torture”

“genitalmutilation”

“egodownharsh”

“othersexualassault”

“totaldarkness”

“constant”

“total”

“fearupharsh”

“weknowall”

“walling”

“constantwhite-noise”

“futility”

“smallbox

confinement”

“icebathstoinduce

hypothermia”

“mockburial”

“visionsandparanoia”

“including”

“thewaterboard”

“silence”

“black-site”

“totheverge ofdeath

andbackagain”

“therepetitionappraoch”

"TheCIAresponded that 'all pain is subjectivenot objective'"

pain to be transmitted, dirt,

t o a b a s e l i n e d e p e n d e n t s t a t e

6.2.1.1: and what Scarry terms the "incontestable reality" of pain, threads
a crossing with the aspect—*gold, gold, red-earth, mirror-bronze*—

of epic-theory called *enargeia* that "bright unbearable
reality"—you feel it, the overwhelm,

in your body, and there is no halt, break, relent, or escape.

c o m p l e t e d a r k n e s s "
" t o t a l "
" c o n s t a n t "
" b l a z e d l i g h t "
" s t e r i l e w h i t e l i g h t "
" c o m p l e t e d a r k n e s s "
" c o n s t a n t "
" w h i t e " " t e r r o r "

*Do you feel it, Diomedes, how all of it is unfolding*
*out under the emergency of darkest night*—dirt-glint, star-wreck.

felt to be possible of lasting beyond the trauma effect of simulated death, I am I did not want to be the long century of

“Theybeat
me
inaway
thatdoes
not
know
any
limits.”

“Therewasblood
allover.
Theycutallover
myprivateparts.
Oneofthemsaid
itwouldbebetterjustto
cutitoff,
asIwouldonly
breedterrorists.”

“Take me to the hollow ships,
or bind me here on this terror-
ground, and test
the information
I have told you of Hector,
and his armies; please
ransom me back to my father,”
Dolon said almost to no one,
no one, or emergent night.

“Icanstillhear
thevoice
ofoneofthe
[prisoners]
inmyhead
askingthem
tostop,
sayingbloodwas
comingoutofhismouth.”

“Iused
myblood
towrite
‘Iam
innocent’
and‘thisis
unjust’
onthewalls
ofmycell”

gold black fire it bronze of

the underlying mechanisms

6.3: That emergent
pain—inside the frame

of the question, brutal
sphinx—is an "obscene

conflation" of inmost
life (call it privacy)

and absolute openness
to the force field

of the world, annulling
both (and personhood)

in that collision, crisis,
and envelopment;

that the archive—
*gold, gold, mirror-*

*bronze*—is glorious
with representaions

that "explore" this—
is the real prisoner's

dilemma of the epic.

*Feel, how in your terror-armor you yourself are emergent*
*night, pure force, and radiant exception in the epic*—

8.0: Law; and bodies; the sum & difference
in the chimera of every living
person; animal; night; film; dirt & syllable;
soundwaves; openenss, and the forming of the senses;
the breath; and sex; the making of the world
in speech, made even at that last inmost limit
of the self; any addressable reality; data;
land; and water; sentences of time both precise,
and indefinite; the space of a cell; a feeding-tube;
your beautiful death; empire, and its myriad
apparatuses, machines & agents; human
and artifical intelligences; the drones
that flyeth by their synthesis; pain;
and the rending of the subject at the traumaeffect:
nothing nowhere that is not weaponized by the epic.

"Forget all ideas of escape, Dolon—
even that last shred of flight in your heart—
for even tho you've given us good intelligence,

I refuse to let you go, because I know
we'd only see you again in combat—[the grasses
wet with it all]—or as a spy among the hollow ships."

this terrible war
you wrote
that seems to go

on forever
it's not fair

(though there's
nothing to that)

that this war
shall take away
all my daughters

one in the drone-
strike in April
then seasons

post-grid
amid the varied
architecture &
geometries

of this last exile
last city of my dis-
appearnce virtual

as in a novel in which
the war goes on

, an emergent kind, albeit lesser, this new lividity, undead, I am I did not want to be detained among the carcinogens, and

| | | |
|---|---|---|
| Out of desperation and a sense of injustice I also went on hunger strike for ten days about three or four weeks after I slashed my wrists” | | Strange music and loud man-made sounds were played around the clock, which in addition to the constant screams of the other prisoners |
| | “Denied in full”<br>“Denied in full”<br>“Denied in full”<br>“Denied in full”<br>“Denied in full”<br>“Denied in full”<br>“Denied in full”<br>“Denied in full” | |
| “Although I was not able to see anything due to the darkness, I was able to smell and taste the blood that was falling down my throat” | | around me made sleeping extremely difficult and very disturbed. When I did manage to fall asleep I often had nightmares” |

els like that constant white noise, naked, enforced, corrosive of the person, strange flora in the flash back “the shit is

6.4: In her treatise on mourning and tragedy, Nicole Louraux argues that AIAI AIAI as a specific cry of pain & dramatic lament carries an anti-political force;

6.4.1: that those syllables AIAI AIAI drawn thru the human person in rising decibles grate against the word for ALWAYS (aei);

6.4.2: ALWAYS ritually invoked to mean the on-goingness of the city and political order, ALWAYS as a claim on forever, claim & will to empire:

" c o m p l e t e d a r k n e s s "
" t o t a l "
" c o n s t a n t "

6.4.2.1: that every & absolute obliteration of any mortal body—*sea-black, firelit bronze, mirror-black, weapon-grade chrome*—which is the pure motive of the epic.

6.4.3: That the cucial abstraction of the body—the cry of pain—calls the political

utterly into question, and that this is done with the lone and chorus

of women's voices is refutation, and first transcednet critique of the epic.

3.1.3:The Loeb renders Dolon's beheading like this: "He spoke, and the other was about to touch his chin with his stout hand and beg him, but Diomedes sprang on him with his sword and struck him square on the neck and sheared off both sinews, and while he was still speaking his head was mingled with the dust."

3.1.3.1: Hobbes, in his retirement, translates the Doloneia like this:

"hurt us [you] cannot if I kill you now.

"As Dolon then beginning was to pray,

"Tydides' sword lighted on's neck so just,

[elision, here, reveals how bare life—not a beautiful death—
is the fate of the common soldier in the epic
out under emergent night          under apartheid          in the colonies.]

"That from his shoulders fell his head away

"As he was speaking, and lay in the dust.

ize—of the underlying mechanisms of how I am in the epic, I am I did not want my pain to be transmitted, dirt-abomina

3.1.3.2: Three centuries later,
three centuries of soveriginity—
*gold, red, chormium, bonze*—brute, dread,
sprawling along a million-million
axes: under such conditions, Oslwad
writes the Doloneia only as a death
to be transmitted—*mirror-bronze*—

“They keep asking him why why

which is the underlying mechanism of the epic.

*You strip him there of the rare,*
*soft, weasel-fur cap,*
*and in your terror-armor*

*this emergent night*
*set out with hate to intensify*
*your ambush theme*—

“He gave away groaning every secret in his body

“And was still pleading for his head

“When his head rolled in the mud.

s the other dead won’t touch the stuff slow boiling pith to pulp, I am I did not want to be asphyxiated, dry submarine, c

kers; the other dead won't touch the stuff, slow boiling pigs to pulp, I am I did not want to be asphyxiated, dry

9.0: That the reckoning tense of language

“ D e n i e d i n f u l l ”<br>
“ D e n i e d i n f u l l ”<br>
“ D e n i e d i n f u l l ”<br>
“ D e n i e d i n f u l l ”<br>
“ D e n i e d i n f u l l ”<br>
“ D e n i e d i n f u l l ”<br>
“ D e n i e d i n f u l l ”<br>
“ D e n i e d i n f u l l ”

can be a counter-force to redaction,

erasure, and obliteration—*gold, red,*

“ b l a c k - s i t e ”<br>
“ w h i t e ” “ t e r r o r ”<br>
“ m o c k b u r i a l ”<br>
" c o n s t a n t "<br>
" t o t a l "<br>
" c o m p l e t e d a r k n e s s "<br>
“ t h e r e p e t i t i o n a p p r a o c h ”<br>
" e m e r g e n t n i g h t "

*mirror-bronze*—is the dream of the book.

the after the airstrike<br>
never leaves your

animal-memory

a kind of determinism<br>
(posthuman there

"in the site<br>
of destruciton "

you wrote)<br>
the man's arm,<br>
the man's<br>
face closeup

of his face with his eyes<br>
covered dissolves

and the shred part<br>
of the voiceover shred

part of the human<br>
animal is

the listening effect<br>
you wrote finally

I heard you say—I am I don't want to be the proof of how it evacuates, shatters, breaks apart levels the built world," and the

9.1: The dream of the book or any speculative language—

9.1.1: any speculative language, practice,

or technology—the body even—

" b l a z e d l i g h t "
" c o n s t a n t "
" t o t a l "

" s t e r i l e w h i t e l i g h t "
" v i s i o n s "
" c o m p l e t e d a r k n e s s "

9.1.1.1: nomadic, improvised, assembeled

against the glaring emergency powers.

" c o n s t a n t n o i s e "
" t o t a l " " h a l l u c i n a t i o n s "
" i n s o c i a l i s o l a t i o n "

" c o u n t e r "
" h o o d i n g "
" i m m o r t a l e p i c "

under the metastais sun

remember the film
of the testimonies
remember the image

of the drone in the rug
remember the dawn-lit

memorial crowd
their keening
the very theorization

and ardor the disaster
requires you wrote

remember me beyond
these last details
and fragements

of a body that has
sufffered remember
the hands touching

folding the shroud
cloth, diaphanous—

*black-basil, dark-blue,*
*oil-black*—

heard you say—I am I don't want to be the proof of how it evacuates, shatters, breaks apart levels, the built, wo

10:

AIAI

aiaiaiaiaiaiaiai
aiaiaiaiaiaiaiai
aiaiaiaiaiaiaiai
aiaiaiaiaiaiaiai
aiaiaiaiaiaiaiai
aiaiaiaiaiaiaiai

N O

X

S U N

*a i a i a i a i*
*aiaiaiaiaiai*
*a i a i a i a i*
*aiaiaiaiaiai*
*a i a i a i a i*
*a i a i*

AIAI AIAI
A I A I A I A I
AIAIAIAIAI
AIAIAIAIAI
A I A I A I A I
AIAI AIAI

## Note on Ambush

—BEGIN PGP PUBLIC KEY BLOCK—
Version: Keybase OpenPGP v1.0.0 | Comment: https://keybase.io/crypto


xsFNBFgHpBcBEAC8oLbIsP6edIqeu6TJU6lWlFFdAhtDMbXsE+xYSRuTIU6I/Idp
ozmd4F1tnmFti3TSob8fhdSsvmdhSubGk8U7iwqONTR5ZkawToiEVgR1QK9YyRAw
rpe6Pvab6ofAIeOoshYWmrufjLhm49z+W4GBcXnlZeZhnPt5o28dTdd5vKB7hquo
Vm1JDUwUXKKXsAKYJEqqoE9Wo99WjLULJtFvlybDU9c+q15xF+cVnzo3XMpczOZ9
PGvH+Ym6m4OOjapcrqfyw/Uy7A1OM1dJxlq4moR9ADef5QSR4Q7Xo34VLQJpAt1l
KSFEJaKVgyDULaEHVnsSnAUuzK+c+ww9dvdxA6e55O9yYDIuzEFKTNPbMUO9NaWM
jfApH+5XWO+xWEU4fsgnNygPeVnfEGFUueqW2rXZcami7hDeVGEcKlWUfQcYpA2K
oEZ+6eDaIOA4/ILdOfT1671cNLSZWqUFkw1uW4uSd+BHxk4xYWLQxwFCpGTV/h+h
PPOe884Kfr2rnUiotAjE11AI9eJXY2PNF93TzYvoyMz8H1AdCsm1aqWds52ynCtJ
R+/JG8xU4Re93CrR4rNh34P8pidUCUt/3ut53kOx9OZo2lhcNoYrfSNhJjGSjM4m
rZOkJa+2XKzORJQ6VdCXJv7Rkd2qVFmtqdQ6ayfYGExjoHdyxxZnVDA2qwARAQAB
zS9KZWZmcmV5IFBldGh5YnJpZGdlIDxqZWZmcGVoaHlicmlkZ2VAZ21haWwuY29t
PsLBbQQTAQoAFwUCWAekFwIbLwMLCQcDFQoIAh4BAheAAAoJEK8jOxB+/j/u/poP
/oJry1u8VnVsJsaGsfzvW3NAathgJzuoJLABzG+DkdFoMvh7nkegnM8gEh+kffFN
3czV74yHv+fs/Ncj2Gys6hzEv9E2Mrip+B/Qy8krBuwUdoKFE6bLPXvsV8ecY/SQ
wiwrwoR3topCL1iK7C/+rZGJB9eDMH7rp1qE5WaNAaodPzXgbOPx1/Caarj+5zgA
qzNiOfdqx5fIl2kgD64G8pLjvos4trKHXLG+ex5AMEkAoSFu6KN8XOSQrQdMh8Tu
rXrUz49BxponmbYfS6qsqJRLpvaaWWFmKvzUH/pleLxaLXAaLX/aMHw6qwSoetb2
3oVvN4HZLKt8JpbQszQYWACfvD2sNwOL6yinHB59RgKz2B3JdACF5RevtF75t92a
rDcFK7td1hWY2dh6Hj83k8ARNzBPWhQ6YQb9ORSHFFzvDHzd2C4Bbo8QqBFvXq5X
7eH5j3PXmYoGclY9jHOfl2qCy44cSpptkgdNL42zc7wDIVDZw9ZbXhbSxiljSH61
6i7EP4vG1uciKAvwvDVos3nTrzaU4MI3PoRSEUP2oTo3nTvy7tIkxyDxMWIdpTIV
hatEkiHlCokeNtG5dlYQRoLvbSyIamSk4ib5s8G6PSMRVY1by9u6mlSUfb8naedA
oM8Uj7/idtH8yBbwWaBQoVTFNEbVpO68ZSgirxxNfz7czsFNBFgHpBcBEAC6+eC7
Q8ejjQCorHgaHrcAplJRoRz2KdyULylMWgotXkaEMWyJE6oa3tMv+QzL/WKqsStb
vi6p5Ns++6hMCE8lqyb//nd+XZqnD7z2Ys+o8NoS/oI/4aqjKddns2QYdar5rJUV
LlXo2jSZ/xQTYQmsJcTJyXO3gbTEP4QCmNPzfKROKG/t/JKN2dPvjYVrsQXFr5gO
gZaLyLX2DUlymFMHvdR52JU4vnXpg3wXlDOYnKQ2No/P11kZdWvI66lzPJxwBd1s

fqcK8V56zThl4xaZV8WFpCjnALngHAHb4mnOd5NNkoeXd3N3aXiddndVfaigoPoC
PE8j9IHqOHGUVy3wah6mZYbHLTcScskq0p79+jazAONLSx8OxHfDjgaZOJKpMHG4
RW90ctnBwvTkJKbQYR7wI6jXDB5Bp83KDalQSvzS2phdfJ4kKopoLOa/fY7hG4lU
jwcmxP57T5A/GWT0DTvZVx71pBzwt1xqh204ef0C4iJOaWTW7l9geW7tT1ChWn+M
8J/B+TEO1OvLlH1s6LeziVmsQfKHt03JGW6DYU+Ia2+52/OS6barKxWFgwov11Tu
9WtwlAUCf3Ou2x/fIjxNzHenQrcLYrrkIM3Ryk8fzX8O308lTKv6yfrR+fgXSrbs
OKyjQldT2datQk2F30e4kuoCKm8Bo6FFsnLZOQARAQABwsOEBBgBCgAPBQJYB6QX
BQkPCZwAAhsuAikJEK8jOxB+/j/uwV0gBBkBCgAGBQJYB6QXAAoJEEvg2bIYE4DF
u6MQAJS8LV8MvL9cydcU8PEtHtnO5Fq3XFbl+hVf8B/qfCMhNh+bdgPeZ7A7LoV5
QK2wUJJSOBwIfNZBFeTY2svKK3+pyGlUJBqy3vn/YPW4CmTUWLsGrO/jpTIgd86u
QHRxNpVp9zls4xJEGNSfoAzWL5i0IGq0XKweKTkzj9NYGM9qs+lbPF8EjM5zDmFt
kXnF0K7WP4TUWlGKFJ1MSMpgA4EqNRYf51fTigk8sipAug00+Jxyqhc1Yp2gYP5J
Z5GXK2Cw9i+R61FAiv2CudgTmQsXUcfcbMFy199RFumf855b5LuoGYByet5c/4qZ
6/35WEfBrC/h95Z/BVbP52x7TPncN7G263wP0njwCEUz2x6NiwdFWGYGfUBJ3nsl
dLMOuYvZZYeSlyyXuVmvgcD8QdTBFfeyZiXJjgfKd2y3l9k47E57CGxlgKKkNOcJ
gcSyDlIYm8H0Kx072AC+SloZQFdIc3w7YiTx3rTuhSqQvlrXnqL9cBxU3czB1P56
c3iHepYcLk4NgjXl8T7ZQf+t2Oq6GDHT+HWKcoEUfiSUuJHY4qtQlxIFgZkRYWnC
4liuuCLWPktr41vcwISm6AODPbhqecf+uow37BJuCScJtj6Dkp6Fh2+TcHNrCBhR
BuztV7bTT7OepWRaNhTae8pd5wV5Zn2NGSZhkYDcmsktD3OE/GYP/i5xNHv5vZOb
CVZgjAHH8YUEIxKcbMtwrYs7Ei1M7ePoDe85ddoxNuXGICVO9SHJNUzXizrxjaxE
fQKkDMN00zvgZdyWOVO+eZGDYd8uasSOg+toxpIAtz4d9EJNEGT7YzgrJj7Gtnnc
IhZuBNoLmEyLZJ9bNLyfYAsjVBA0ic5fzQNupqzItkgUve4LMbW0RODZod/ZGcJG
VoH55X3YTvnnCIu3aCQ8Q/xcV16Ae/R3m/r7m2hfKeTOL9MNTkkKBWu16tqsM1kE
mTwldErlBkQ/XRin+yk77/G3AJhvL1y95WUk4EbpaMlAaO1bhZycASFVnRMPjWrc
1ujYdoduzZRZfPMgbmz2co2ORFlbRxLazySNhi1rs6IPpXKnqn908/7xlDuNPZHZ
bqOL+nWrVHimd4M69tjFLMhAbqZtnOnD3Y8LBZ8OmZntLsY+wXZvUATBmXU3I399
+N5ZXqooI7Hg7KMsWgnaajCHDLtu2hLtXWy4YcCjYeXl6SzDl6fR9y8n31bXdFjq
NJg/7x8hoFq7LM7e87Z5TMmKbfslhTWeI6pPgfGkQWdn8XnuiwiInxZFC1xI4G3l
SBWcpFS1QO8XjVYa8XJz9aDtQBKvokCPb4gyE826R0pamTDShta4ZE4BzQpsz+yr
9J4XJCu2tvBf4Pwjo F8dSU4isyamiXIGzsFNBFgHpBcBEADKJBsYegIFuREZKoCS
QKGgmWSskoSprgmxSiAG7jqVqTD8cpwvG6Tctr6jwzl8/W75uEWzWDQL9noOGaFP
J8VljJ4G2JAuEh7csD1arYt3tNF8LXDQprYCwUqlbYG1a//uHyv4gGH44r2w7sOx
KL28khoPSnBDBQ2p6+n7JwjZisfh57PX0AhBrKoOeuaZZTFIzs1AohIpNfEPKiOo
NjicraMh5GaxRryDqPcQRJmaN04pzrK004S8uI730hV6+uNn0x7615vClbDxWHut

gJZYTnUFOoEaMYyXNGgEVrDw9uvsVrujK8gi4EAAQRpHvTHFs6RjLTRhwEikD/r/
Jpd+1qjQLjCYVmEUFLMFWkrcfHcTjBD8ta3osmHURW1ZnbiRdmuIlFMbjqafmRmm
FNva3wIIaqowOIder/lOKu29Y8/5VDFZY/c+vesjgQfLlPXse/kXzX2/8Wrk1p5y
TxxFXqMX+aA4K+U1KIflA1nGJn/Z2ZOpN/elH/5TJfU3Ys2VTLh42/WhRBv3BU+X
pAvfme1cVctmoVqjY3vwgjEjjDpQIx/Ia4TDHFqK2vcABt3wUwOxZk8JnPxpVRx8
wuQ2V7miRwzFmtOFyeMdp/zqDvGVJ9KWEQ3jbcBH5Ry7Mm+MlRwJdG3sjO4XKCL1
xZ4GdKNl3z2msSY5tGpsPgG4OQARAQABwsOEBBgBCgAPBQJYB6QXBQkPCZwAAhsu
AikJEK8jOxB+/j/uwVogBBkBCgAGBQJYB6QXAAoJEE34G3kExdqajycQAMRQSHNe
GTAlc4I6oooQNe9kf5rL9vBzx/gl7pIvWIGN1R/KCifcRknrzVRGif2pMF3BAlgS
2p+WyEK87CdlR7rRXJq5toP6nPfdVVE2jSsKnzBTNMfociRv3ebFq24hokSKoE9C
Y5p9F2kRu/NJvN3AJlflLaHliBildk+kHypYAxdXYmu1HOSMaELQoWU5WfIsoE2H
H+TITXSXixcuFENhu1jovdvZDJDtOI4GE5ne6M1xfh9yzObiRy3EqU6AqGOGyRs5
q7c2Mqr74hd7AV4RslNxfyp54AZXTTnwto7ifGmLLQaEahS8eePaLhr2ZsMbO9BK
aRCLAVtsg2HYcuOnwzLA355oUB4agC31G8kloO51d8wI4rduKOLscmXXqP3/o34a
DcH/O+wAUcpUJgyakSctiwzeD9BmomPHAEG+S1Vu1919bCyONuEghL4nUC2KLSDu2
RAT45fL2bsZzkvqV1mrth8GuqMHzDhjR6NKkJlIY++3h4iS/jmzjMKT2hDKACf3U
LCfrsu+oqi3aujuX+OiOhWxdICkx2oyhECJ3q14GotDy5kQCWvHphEkzOoEc3bUT
tmDh4teK4feJoJeHSLJFS9yEugqPzJPlUGrv8TgPtPgt7WXBNfU78ve6nPoXXV+D
MkzHa4+pCG9WfuoiqoofmA++upWUUzN4WNPNAWQQAJqQbV7KT6MNEx+z67TrS5ve
fH9ixjh/tpv2E/+kVjzr7EukvrWHZ/3sm5izm7I4ktRO9a/LLl/Nlvrqoho7YRGA
EiF8oMOA+Fa5gZHk7QDZfEr2Pnn1lkANwHnyLpDpI5KV9wACVrLo92A5aBoGBYIo
LDIXWIEYQOOo+RRNweh7oS9vSEYaiH21jD9+Np5Lv515fWoCcCFrzK3+RbNlsKef
Hasb4ThwsnPeSxQTz6kPEmQmKaktHk8f2iWjHjs9DAUKwcAX3KqlDBnz4O9Z+kf+
ihATQhbSzUklz23r6DNHO2w3wd2Crjv6b2JSXYswCYvH72tZK4Sbleg5SUGnRJV7
ihfKmNIQtJAcRTGKEzybQ2pao6EZefSb9Xaoju42jcUDoJ7wNNJtu1le+cnAsQXN
haccAJGlYS9BlPFbqulAVrRTLExiFHYOUP9SK7c4Qj8Xu3Vl+8KT4GYIF6IZSf6y
gg55x/OGJzOS7EAoU4t+/lohmP6To9hCvVkq+3qCnyBgmAVjIuD/1REQFWavUu4V
xp+LrukSP27fsTjO58tKb+y4czC3wwhUtV7DUeoznvegzjGFFAAEbmrCLfRZsXhn
7WBtumoXNvXtghAOVRWnRHsh8DiE8rOiuFtdy+XNAmEFqC35I/xFW7i8fzDtQgEW
rWZC5tUoR6TUYzU3FpKi
=GJNB

-----END PGP PUBLIC KEY BLOCK-----

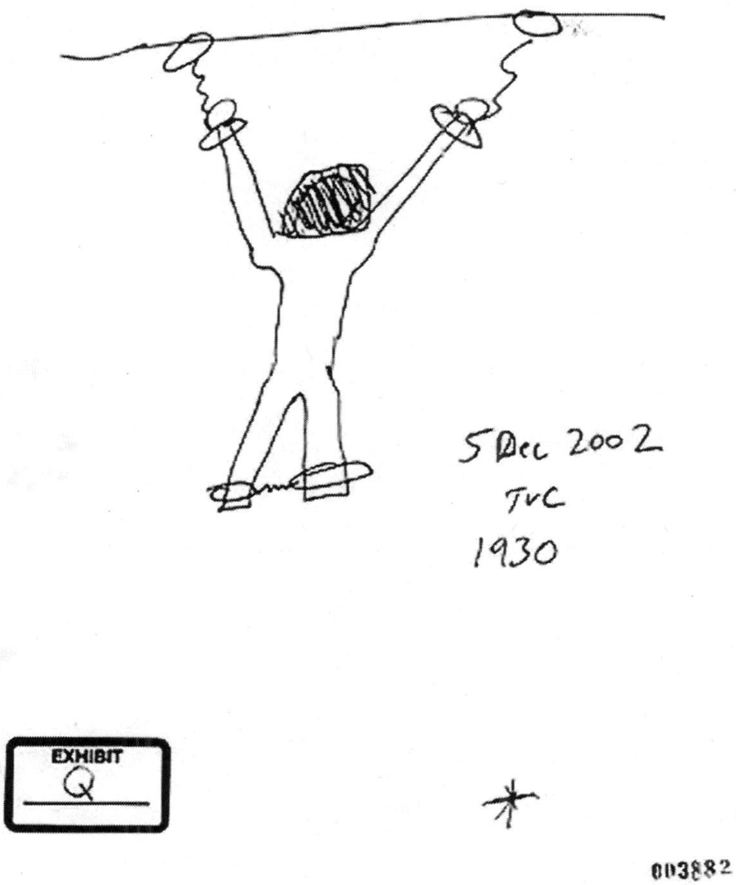

include wings of screamings that are strained to sharp points / include his wings of sharpstretched lament / his arms / include *Allah* / he cried *Allah* / the 22-year old taxi driver / he cried / may I cling to selfish ease / or dishonor my father by restraining / the wings of shrill lamentation / he cried for hours / cried *Allah* / sharpstrained *Allah* / to cage the wings of lamentation / he was caged / he was sharpstretched / a stress-position the experts call it / to make him cry his wings of *Allah* / strained to sharp points / they beat him / they walled him / they drove their knees into his thighs over 100 times / they beat his thigh muscles into a kind of jelly / he weighed 122 pounds / his legs / read the autopsy report / would have needed to have been amputated / had he survived / he cried / how can I dwell here *Allah* / in peace if I restrain / my piercing sorrow's wings / and dishonor my father *Allah* / he cried / sharpstrained *Allah* / my cries are wings / they pierce the cage / my cries arrows / they fly / by sorrow's / intelligence

# In The Epic

O for the muse of atropine, for the muse of the CWC (singing since '93), for the genius (and beauty) of human reason
and not the video of inspectors in hazmat suits taking samples from the aftermath of the colorless, odorless, weaponiz

"The day is a dragon, and images / of the city's ruin glide over the gross / orb of its eye: where walls remain their graffit
whole neighborhoods have no heat-signatures. // The Seer's warning ignored; the King is / a figment of sectarian heroi

Under a crisis sun; a collateral sun; a white phosphorous sun rockets the city, then the gif of its 5000 degree pyrophori
its repetitions; or the sun is a vortex; a vehement sun finding its victims everywhere; a tragic sun crying *aiai aiai aiai*; a

You haven't been here before, this deep in the earth; it's 1970, Iphigenia, and you're just a rabbit in a cage,
carried through the warehouse of shells and canisters to check for leaks, your respiratory system, the arming-theme of

"Engines! / All I / hear are engines." // "Polynices advances leading / a column of foreign fighters; he is / his own imag

"Thinking," the philosopher says, "must begin with the catastrophe, the corpse, *human* ultimately comes from the Lati
And altogether elsewhere a detainee is stripped, confined to a box, then shovel by shovel—shown the limits of the hu

I am Yasser Talal Al-Zahrani, my name is Rachel, I was discovered at 12:39, they attached wires to my toes, they say th
did not want my name to be transmitted, I am Joan of Arc, later they cut out my throat, they catalog my image, my sh

a disaster sun; a sun / over the city like emergency / powers, and his sun-green blotter / afterimage; an Ashura sun, red,
sounds; a vortext of future griefs, the sun / that will be written; the hundred names / of the sun, and history loud with

Over the thigh-tall grass, red with it all, sallies the ballad of first collision: the city out of some swarded vision, beside
river, we thought could be the start of something free, now pure territory and proliferation in the force-fields of the e

Without memory and universalism—greenest in the body politic, and hoisted as a voice, sail, and final treaty
of the person in that post-war (utopian) document The Universal Declaration of Human Rights—there can be no resis

"O you city / of daughters, keep / quiet, for your / crying will suck / the heart from our fighters / who go to repel //
his rush. I am / a power myself. / There will be no / Damascus that is / not mine."

Under the trees around the capitol, I got to rest my weekend nudity, sated from a larger ration of bacon fat and cornm
then two ripe peaches I traded for, angling all my limbs for August...and before Antietam, mud-dark, prophetic that c

Had a dream the suicides stopped, had a dream all their limbs grew back while they dreamed, had a dream they desert
but lazy, loafing, an army of lovers angling all their limbs toward the light in August, a whole sprawling empire of their

"Eteocles you will / not listen, because I / am your sister. / Brother, the city is / speech, made by each / speaking one to

The lyric/anti-lyric seam: thrilling to run your voice along it, become a wave of affect, be its renunciation too—and th
before the ancient image of the fighter's body pierced by javleins, thrilled (the verb is critical, is the double-bind) by t

“Thus the roll call of death should always be taken as it was first taken by Homer in the record of war that stands at the beginning of western civilization. Here each death, whether (‘freight… pon… th… of the… kysite… of e… in four aspects: the name each…

ı disarmament,
d epic.

// tells the civil war; craters; smoking tanks; / fighters in soccer jerseys with RPGs; / poisoned,
:s; / and we, sorry chorus to this history.”

ity—not merely circulating this white phorphorous sun; a time-image sun, the unendurability of its rays,
d you looking up for an abolitionist sun, its light to wave agitate agitate; then no sun at the blank totality of the epic.

sarins’s epic.

nary, blazoned, / flying a glowing martyr-poster:

ı *humus*, the earth, the burying ground.”
an—thrown under the twelfth technique of the epic.

will rape me, there was a camera there, I am I
me, they archive it, I am proof of the epic.

/ ecstatic; the sun a rush of vowels and liquid /
ıem.”

ıe silver-green
ic.

ance against the epic.

al,
ek, some American epic.

d, a standing army no longer, professional no longer,
efusals, a dream to end the epic.

Letter on Mark-Making & the Attack of Song: *I’m writing this one longhand involved in the rhythms of making marks, so forgive my terrible handwriting. (M already in the street, in the train station, and somewhere else I can’t remember, I th in the flow of the city, and staring straight at me like I was a camera, and you start the wake, a feeling of saying yes to future searches, future disappearances, and that we’re reduced to letters again already, can’t believe that I’m writing you from this city-idyl like nowhere else: the day just glides along from gleis to gleis, glides on gla polyglot and efficient, and because to be an immigrant is to be marked for kontrolle bass-sound of the banker’s city. I’ve been listening to the isolated vocals track of “Gi the song when Merry Clayton starts the chorus of ‘Rape! / Murder! / It’s just a sho you hear against the blank sound of no-music, how the attack of song makes the wo terrifying; it’s full of transport, maybe even a kind of anagogy, and yet it’s still utte with the work of the negative, and I know you know this, it’s how resistance radic question is how to sustain radicalized being over / through / against time, how to h antagonism? In your last letter, you asked what images have stayed with me, which presence, that keep making me their imaginary: a time-lapse map of every protest Missile Command (do you know that video game), the present and recent past are Istanbul seen from a distance, and lit up from its own protest fires; a memory of a c bits & scraps of colored film are added to the air, and for a second the fighters think then they realize that the shattered colors are the fragments of the Rainbow Bridge January walking in Boston, in the middle of an intense snowstorm, I suddenly hal storm that image has rhymed with winter in my mind; and you, I keep seeing you was staring straight into a camera; then a river, the wide mud-dark river, America go to hell.” I’ll give a Zürich wall the last word:* kill the cop / in

another. // Don’t you see, death can’t be— / look at the buses filled / with corpses—Eteocles, death / can’t be our city’s / politics.

sort of advanced art you go in for Dr Pethybridge, and with a kind of arrogance, pride at singing the double-bind. And it all hap
cast of them, his throat their quiver of likenesses you thrill at his destruction—your ticket to the heights—which is the first id

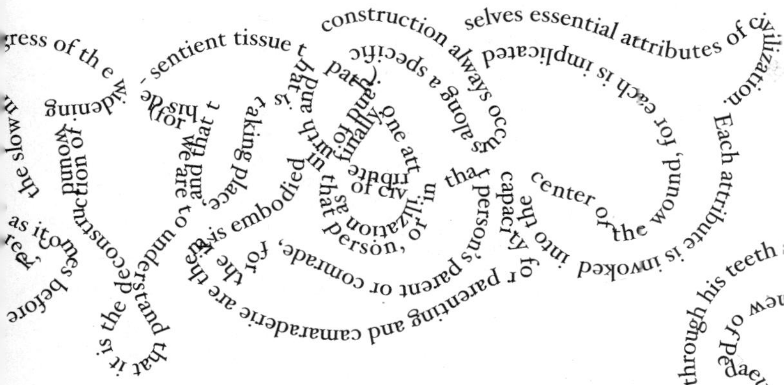


*-ded to get away from the screen, and I wanted to be*
*-pe it up, or make a fair copy later). A few times*
*-w you, for a moment, just standing absolutely still*
*-nto it, then gone. And each time the same feeling in*
*-d with those losses, those labors. I can't believe that*
*end of the alphabet. Zürich does the summer*
*-zelight, glides all the way to glücklichkeit; it's*
*police' is scrawled all over Zürich, it's the*
*-ter," and there's this moment—the 2:48 mark—in*
*it's just a shot away,' and when it's just the vocals,*
*-otest, at once absolutely beautiful, and yet still*
*in the struggle of the Here & Now. It's the same*
*-g—it's like a holy transfiguration, almost. But the*
*-ack of song day by day by day, to live that beautiful*
*-ppeared. Here are a few that keep exerting their*
*-ld since 1979, the protests flare up like explosions in*
*radical; the Death Vally star-field; a photograph of*
*battle-scene in New York, it's snowing and slowly*
*weird confetti or something—they're at a loss, but*
*thought of that image for years, and then this past*
*the air to fill with rainbow flak, and ever since that*
*here at the crossing- station looking at me, as if I*
*-nd a voice-over of Huck saying: "All right, then, I'll*
-nct and / in yourself!! *Love. J.*

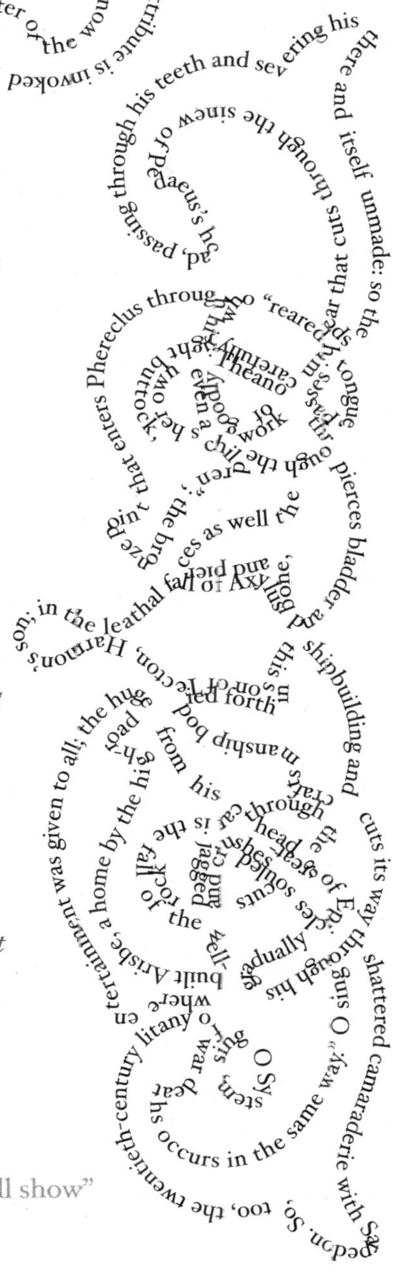


you / have no city, / listen." // "The event will show"

-me-lapse: you before the open book,
epic.

## Force Drift

I know the call for a court is still the enemy—

enemy, too, the longing for a truth

commission, that political imaginary
of a future less vivid
(and the violence
in that deferral).

And what's the sublime halt
and reckoning now—
*blue, black, mirror-bronze,*
*weapon-grade chrome*—now against THE ENEMY
OF MY ENEMY OF MY ENEMY IS...

that grammar of syzygy,
and logic-chain of the State, of the great chain of being,

of Father Saffron, The Rebarbative,
Who Throws His Voice Around

like a statement from the underside
of modernism (pink teeth in its victims):

so the new methodology—the emergent kind—

of the corpse poem, pink teeth in its dead mouth.

# Force Drift

Of the corpse poem, pink teeth in its dead mouth——*black, red, bronze, gold-black, dark red, brown, gleaming, red, yellow-chrome, fire-lit, bronze*——of the underlying mechanisms of how I am in the epic, I am I did not want my pain to be transmitted, dirt abomination, the bitten symptom—park grayed by paper-ash and carcinogenic dust—pink teeth, a sign in the mouth, me and the wasps paper-makers, the other dead won't touch the stuff, slow boiling pith to pulp, I am I did not want to be asphyxiated, dry submarine, dirt submarine, swarming with the casualties, of or through metastasis, and the underlying phenomenon is still awaited, an emergent kind, albeit lesser, this new lividity, undead, I am I did not want to be detained

among the carcinogens, and the school of americas, the number of breaths you can absent under the waterboard, and the twelfth technique, false burial, bite on that, video-taped, analog like any animal or city,so it can be destroyed, effaced, "I trust that Simon's intention is to witness something," I heard you say of or through metastasis [*as they enter the performance space, audience members are each given a shred of car tire to hold, a token of entrance and passage; rubber is burnt throughout; a montage of blasted cityscapes is projected throughout the space and plays on a loop*],
like any acid or school of americas, I am I did not want my naked sex to die in under the second device of simulated death, that will not be torn out of mind, Guantanamo, [*and when the maximum decibels of Skinny Puppy subside, only once or twice, a minimal composition plays as relent, relent must be felt to be possible* *o f*

[illegible]

[illegible]

simulated death,       I am I did not want to be the long century of it, the school of the Aleph, bare life, digital, sexually humiliated, naked, "constant white noise, no talking, everyone in the dark with the guards wearing a light on their [psychological] heads...." of or through metastasis, and Simon's intention to witness something," I heard you say—I am I do not want to be the proof of how it evacuates, shatters, breaks apart levels the built world," and the underlying—it's not a mechanism, the ground-form of the person, think we must, I heard you say under the carcinogens, and the second device, the other dead won't touch it,       r a i n f a l l (nuclear), low apartment buildings sheared open to the gun-wrecked air—*pink,* [teeth]

[illegible]

*black* [sunlight], *silver, gray,* [air], *weapon-grade chrome*—throat       throated, that constant white noise, naked, enforced, corrosive of the person, strange flora in the flashback       "this shit is everywhere," and the excruciating plastic of the feeding-tube in cases, before they removed the throat,    obey, disobey, I was I am not a thing world," and the underlying mechanism, the ground-form, think we must, I heard you say under the carcinogens, and the

to be torn out of mind, a thing torn out at the traumaeffect, I heard you say "we know all," through metastasis, I am not that Gul Rahman, I was I am not that Yasser Talal Al-Zahrani, not that Riyadh the facilitator, I was I am not that mujahideen,  there are no records (a trace) that attest, false burial, to be black sunlight leveling

the built world, streets sheared, throated, thinking the metastasis of the disaster, dirt abomination, and not its relent, not what I thought would it be—*gleaming, red, yellow-chrome, gold-black*—and it smelled like  tea under the dome, I only felt it once [*a chorus of women, some dressed in white, some in black move throughout the performance space, they improvise dances, and sometimes ululations, in response to the musics, and images being projected]*—strange flora in the flashback  in which I am  a person of strange flora, earth—*black, red, bronze, gold-black, dark red, brown*—body, dirt network, sprawling, excruciating through the flashback, a remnant like any animal remade at the traumaeffect, the long century of it, underneath it, a silhouette on the earth where the city used to be, white strange flowers, a trace of the city wall, mural flowers, sprawling rhizomatically—all through the school of americas, that cruel metastasis—not what I thought it would be, dirt submarine, I am not that Yasser, not mujahideen, before they removed the throat, ginger, pink teeth, irises,

[illegible]

[*intermittently throughout the ritual a woman, or whole chorus will approach an audience member, establish some kind of connection, or gestural accord, and as these relationships evolve, and ultimately find their durational shape, the chorus will whisper a message to the audience member (themselves now an integral part of the rites), and this is the sign that the ritual has ended for this person, and they leave, and it is understood that the'll keep the message, as a private token of passage, and exit back into the sudden, and catastrophic world.*] pink rigor paper makers, the other dead won't touch the stuff, slow boiling pith to pulp. I am I did not

[illegible]

absent under the waterboard, and the [illegible] false burial, bite on that, video-taped,

[illegible]

metastasis [illegible] I don't want to

world," and the underlying mechanism, the ground-form, think we must. I heard you

say under the carcinogens, and the second device, the other dead won't touch it,

[illegible]

the second device, the [illegible] low

*black [sunlight], silver, gray, weapon grade chrome* throat throated, that constant white

[illegible]

absent under the waterboard, and the [illegible] false burial, bite on that, video-taped,

[illegible]

world," and the underlying mechanism, the ground-form, think we must. I heard you

say under the carcinogens, and the second device, the other dead won't touch it,

[illegible]

*black [sunlight], silver, gray, weapon grade chrome* throat throated, that constant white

nuclear rainfall, eyes, irises, and plastic sandbags, rubber, cords, wires,
low apartments throated, streets torn out at the disastereffect, a t r a c e , an
afterimage already even before they removed the throat, underneath it, a
person remade at the traumaeffect, a person of strange flora, and dirt,
earth, c o l o r slides of it, this burial piece—*gold-black, red, yellow-chrome, bronze,*
*dark red, brown, gleaming*—slick, chthonic now as if that were a solution, bare life,
n o s u n l i g h t underneath the twelfth technique, I am I did not want, earth,
I am not bare life, I heard you say through metastasis, the other dead won't
touch it, this paper effect, and intention to witness something, I am not that
remnant, e a r t h , e a r t h , not that pain to be transmitted, the long
century of it, chthonic now, no sun light, earth, earth, e a r t h ,
swarming with the causalities, e x c r u c i a t i n g a l l through the flashback,
[*and now a chorus approaches you, and you find yourself taken up into the sensuous and*
*gestural accord, that project of the human, you move through the dance, then one of the*
*chorus, whispers to you a sentence of perfect secrecy*], in a long century of dirt.

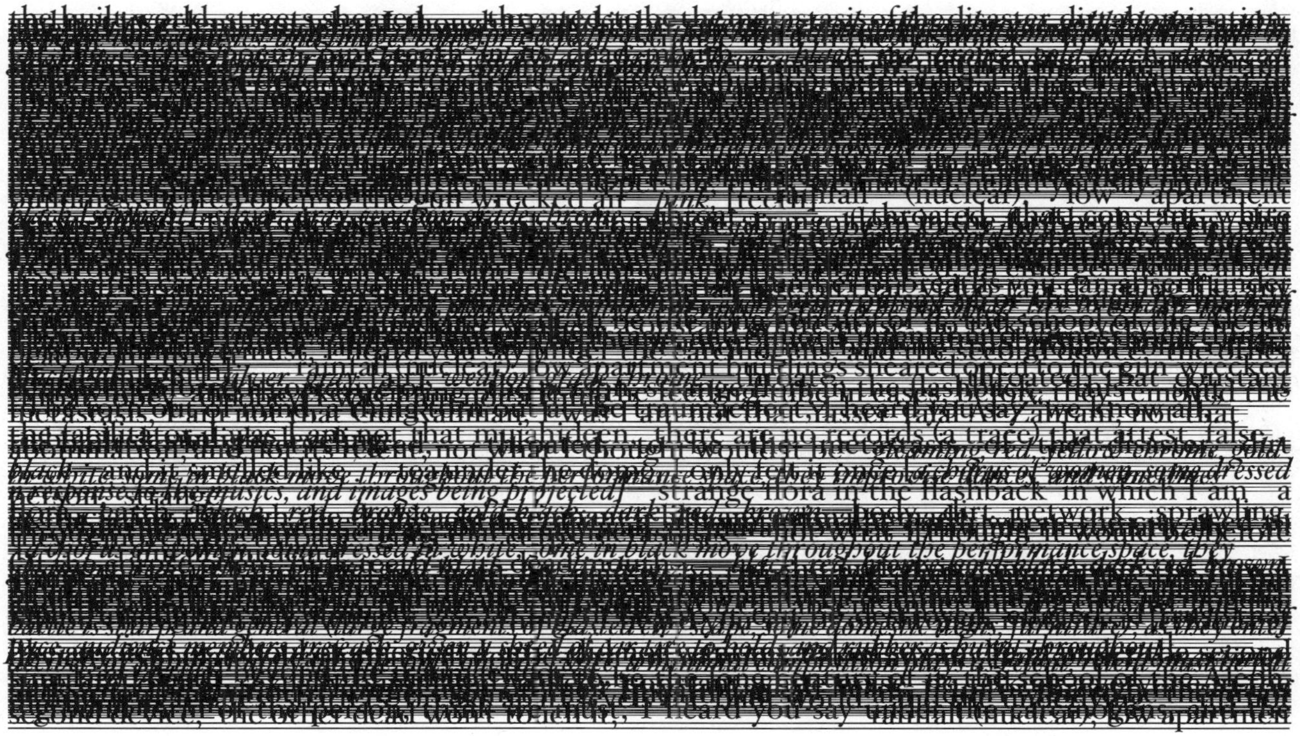

*black [sunlight], silver, gray, weapon-grade chrome*—throat throated, that constant white

world and the underlying mechanism, the groundform, think we must, I heard you

say under the ... and the second device, the other dead won't touch it,

world and the underlying mechanism, the groundform, think we must, I heard you

say under the ... and the second device, the other dead won't touch it,

I don't want to

world and the underlying mechanism, the groundform, think we must, I heard you

*black [sunlight], silver, gray, weapon-grade chrome*—throat throated, that constant white

pain to be transmitted, the ... ness something, I am not that remnant, ... earth, earth, ... not that the power of                                the common s~~trength~~

disrupt          ~~basic~~

the Republic          of

control

branches     ~~h~~as     the

negative          to this structure

portions

The power of the commons disrupts
The Republic of Control, branches
as the negative to this structure, portions
power—as intended of justice. A few years later
I recognized the epic is the world.

*Power*

as intended

of
Justice                    a few years later

I
“recognized

‘the          ~~foreign~~ p~~olicy~~ [is]

the     world.”

# MURAL

*—a future city*

## *g a t e*

Like an exploded dreadnaught, the brutalist architecture of it suspended in midair, as if the film stopped, time stopped, crazy shadow fretwork thrown everywhere under the insurgent sun. A maze of silos and bunkers, strange flora from the flashback grown rampant & feral: flowering, toxic weeds all thru the exclusion zone. A portal & array like a giant lotus seedpod, you touch it, it's livid with the event, growing there. Like a coral colony, spawning and reaching and barring entrance to the city along its sixfold symmetry. A counter-sky of web-like rigging & scaffolding, radiant beams & spires—*gold, red, silver, bronze, bronze, mirror-bronze*—sprawling over the minefields. Concentric rings of locks and watchtowers: graffiti & murals omnipresent, painted, overwritten, on all the concrete and cor-ten surfaces, a circuit of palimpsests—passwords hidden throughout. A swarm of drones, microscopic, nano-scale, sphinx models moving along the seam of criticality (as starlings once did), you breathe in your own (dis)possession. Like the simplest steelwork arch, diaphanous sail and no flag no flag no flag—*gold, red, chromium*

## *passages*

I'm going to argue against amnesty.

I'm going to argue for a reckoning of our cruelty, for a rigorous accounting of the
torture program, its agents and its authors.

I'm going to argue for an image, a memorial, something more than, something
slower than the photograph, which we gloss through its proliferation,
and which then gets archived, filed away, even as evidence, not forgotten
exactly, but unsubstantiated?

I'm going to argue for monumentality,                    for a monumentality equal to
the enormity of it all

*—you can't skip over like a catalogue of ships*

seven murals one
seven murals two
seven murals three
seven murals four
seven murals five
seven murals six
seven murals seven

She stands
on a wall

amid
the ruined
scape.

Her unveiled hair
(as long
as the street
itself )

and an equal
wave of roses

flow in arabesques,
flow into abstracts

replacing the crisis
sun: The Salient,

Which Is Rampant
With Claws,
a lion

leaping onto prey.
History is a sequence

of dying physicalities—
it goes: loud      quiet      loud.
Martyred, her nimbus

is the negation
of emergency powers.

The problem of force,
Simone Weil says,

is in its transformations:
man to lion, victim

to corpse.
Her quiver of grenades
rocket      loud quiet loud      against
The Seated King, against
The Bully, against

The Big-Bellied, The Brute,
The Humiliator, who uses
rape as a weapon of war

(also said of the epic),
Whose Teeth Are
Interlaced, against

The Mercenary,
Whose

Coat
Is
The
Color
Of
The
Surface
Of
The
Earth—
*gold,*
*red,*
*chromium*—

over which her
arrows fire          arrows

that flieth by
struggle's intelligence

# *gate*

As in decisive moment photography—instant—as when the body, “when the formulation of the body as proof returns,” the body moving—*white leopard, red-sepal, fierce-chrome, weapon-grade chrome*—in time-lapse from animal to anima, animus of the political animal in situ as stasis, as civil war—strange flora throughout the channel-locks, through which passage runs, through which you must trespass (strange flora and corpse language overgrowing this burial-piece), you *white leopard, red-sepal* you out among the testimonies, moving, incomprehensible—elsewhere: proliferation & escalation throughout the barrens, the long century of dirt, insurgents wandering or detained, the messenger’s speech calls them *den apatiska,* the apathetic, they wear all black in some regions, wear all white in others, research suggests that cult sect is marked by these differences—their rite incites the start of return, the memory of impossible return in quiet pantomime (instant), as in alif, as in abolish, as in the body is not proof—final treaty of the person, as you, *white leopard* you, *red-sepal* you, *weapon-grade* out among the will to regime—Kontrol suspended, forever in the decisive instant, your eyes now radical organs, eyes struck out like this, like this—*gold, red, bronze, bronze, fierce-chrom*e you—

## *passages*

When I say mural,  I mean when image, writing, and the city are one.

When I say mural, I mean social sculpture, I mean the necessity of that postwar
concept, I mean an image of time we can call postwar, (and really mean it).

When I say mural, I mean *escrache*, I mean the necessity of that post-genocide
practice, I mean the necessity of [the human] being post-genocide.

When I say mural, I mean the state put to the test, the concept of the state,
and its limits, overturned

*—thrown under the abolitionist sun,*
*its light to wave agitate agitate*

seven murals one
seven murals two
seven murals three
seven murals four
seven murals five
seven murals six
seven murals seven

THE BEGINNING OF THE WAR WAS SECRET / she graffitied, all along the broad avenue / the war now public af— / *palm-light, indigo-skinned, mirror bronze*— / "they were some of the worst weeks of the century," / gun noise measures 130 decibels, / battering down a door, a s in the thousand raids, close to 100 / a long century of arrests / and seizures, intensifications of discipline / she wrote "I dreamed this two headed serpent / crossing white sands (las cruces, I think) / cobra-hooded—*black, brown, bronze, gold-black, dark red, / gleaming red, wet red, fire-lit bronze, dark earth*— / and so alien to the environment / —I knew this intuitively—the two headed snake / it was crossing over to me, middle distance.... / I woke before it reached me, at a loss / for what it was an allegory," / "at the beginning" "events were falsified / through terror," on the chords of the bridge / crossing into the city, she graffitied: / —THE MARVELOUS PHENOMENON OF THAT BIRD / SACRED TO THE SUN AND CALLED THE PHŒNIX / APPEARED IN EGYPT AND THE EMPIRE ENDED— // —IS JUST GOING TO BE LIKE THIS— / rivering, repeating the length of the opposite chord, / "at the anniversary of the treason" / the mural is painted, fugitively, throughout the city, / elsewhere in the city, / a dawn ceremony is performed / collectively (in sight of water) / and more precarious, ephemeral / memorials are also enacted, / emergent conditions, and the possibility— / *palm-light, indigo-skinned, mirror bronze*—of a century / not slaughter to Father Saffron, The Difficult, / al-Haysam, The Destroyer who uses / genocide as a weapon of dominion, and "falsified / through terror," she wrote: "the future / is a chimera"—*palm-light, indigo-skinned, / mirror bronze gold-black, dark red, gleaming red, wet red*— / "serpent, sun phoenix—third-world—a kind of anti-epic, / all grafted onto the lions' body, / a kind of anti-griffin—how long the memory / & grammar of the State will persist." / [fragment in a notebook] / Strange flora all throughout / my flashback dreams of that season. / The season, militarized by decibels, / prison dogs barking registers in the nineties, / the night a sentence, and pain-scale—the dogs / are barking at you now, and you cannot run— / the season of the thousand raids—*gold, red chromium.*

## *g a t e*

"We name the mechanisms" empire, and empire—*gold, red*, [imperium]—into which everything flows w/o escape or halt—"is it just going to be like this"—graffitied all over the quarter) everything flows through the latest inventions in violence, and the traumaeffect, irrecuperable passage, that cannot be transmitted, "I come from a country where the person was not given back," post-human now among the pigeons of Zanzibar, "a ghost walking" as tomorrow will be, tomorrow is a lie, and limit, which the twelfth technique weaponizes, and the breaths you can absent under the emergency powers——"irreparable as APOLLO"—of simulated death, you are you, irreparable, and cannot be transmitted cannot halt the gate is five story glass steelwork aviary, lousy w/ machine-insects and chemical agents—*gold, red, chromium, bronze, bronze, fire-lit bronze, blue*——

*passages*

When I say mural I mean, how the film overtakes the building as it's projected on the building.

When I say mural I mean the square occupied with dream of the square—when the street, that first theater and dance floor, remembers itself, precisely through this dream life, remembers the victims of the vehement sun

—*red in the shadow, the living thread*

seven murals one
seven murals two
**seven murals three**
seven murals four
seven murals five
seven murals six
seven murals seven

And did not want my name
to be transmitted (colony

after colony) rendered ex-
traordinarily through imperial

airspace—*gold , black, mirror-bronze, red*—
cubist—*ivory-black*—mural-figure

blasted, keening through the gelatin-
silver print detail, then cut to the end-

stop of the film, the flag all of the screen—
*gold, red, black*—the fasces reversed,

then her flag abolish "total,
complete, absolute," and the forest

of Kalashnikovs, she stands
at the treeline, hair comicbook

medusa down to the martyr-poster's
ground, where it touches it ramifies

techno-organically—*gold-black*
*mirror-bronze, weapon-grade chrome*—

with distances to the free cities
dates   sieges   occupations   detainees,

numbers for divination and survivance
"no symptoms of suicide were dis-

covered on her person"—final
treaty—or in her writing that was dis-

information—*of fire, of without end,*
*of how would you          escape*—

# *gate*

Everything flows: invisible, into a zone of concealment, socially veiled, segregated, into the place that is no-place: the black site prison torture room. The same industrial  logic obtains for the slaughter floor—you where you cannot look,      you  have  no  power. American Sphinx, Who Eats Until He Chokes (also said of the epic), Whose Hair Gets Thicker When He's Mad, Who Disregards The Rights of Others, Who Sinks Deeper Inside His Victims, Who Doesn't Care What Happens, The Unwelcome Sight, The Tyrant, The Colossus looms there at the edge of the city,    a statue-garden & gate like the world-system itself: sudden, catastrophic, invisible, everything flowing—*gold, red, chromium, weapon-grade bronze*— What, o women of Troy,         for a politics of seeing that is not surveillance—*He cried Allah, Allah and yet.*

*passages*

seven murals one
seven murals two
seven murals three
**seven murals four**
seven murals five
seven murals six
seven murals seven

the body tracks in history—
*gold-black, dark red, brown*—

animal led to transgress—*mirror-*
*bronze*—the body open relentlessly

yet the body   yet the gesture
of her body crosses over to you

archaic trace in the capital-
ocene   the wall is an epitaph

after she presses, drags her arms—
*dark red, wet-red*—into marks   she exits

to when the open may yet escape—
*red, gold, mirror-bronze, weapon-grade*

*chrome*—grasses,   grasses—*glittering*—
beyond  the city ringed by earthworks

an epoch of crowds & executions
the moment of looking is an arrest

the long century of it  to withstand
waiting  like the concrete abstract

at once ark/eye/wing  and graffitied:
*Ana, is it just going to be like this—*

exclusion zones (weird flora everywhere
flourishing)—*dark red, wet-red*—the body

relentlessly open to seizure like this
like this—*red, gold-black, mirror-bronze*—

### *gate*

A labyrinth called the Martyrs Gate:
propaganda, and funerary posters paper the fifty-
foot walls, ancient ginkgo groves all along the
outskirts, layers and layers of natural-occurring fog
further out—holograms, or hallucinatory figments
of the fighters are seen throughout the terrain,
broke loose from the collective grief "at approach, or
embarkation," she wrote "it's uncanny, you feel
as if you should be already among their number, the
dead to whom we owe this last shred of the city,"
that was before her rendition, before the purge was
general, when there were yet *targets*, "bodies
in history,"the monographs called the phenomenon,
and its representations, meaning mere, meaning
subject, *thrown under,* and together (one is not one)
in the cell, against the black site techniques, into
the devastating sea—*blue, green, silver, gold, red,*
*mirror-bronze, green, indigo-skinned*—waves waves
waves—at approach or embarkation, one is one, and
not one, fugitive (if that is the correct translation)
all along the ~~path~~ fire that never flags nor sets,
there is no way around only through [your beautiful
death]—*gold, red, red, chromium, weapon-grade*
*bronze*

*passages*

When I say mural I mean that somewhere else entire, a feeling of—*and yet*—
surface that is also limit, enfolded among the disciplines.

When I say mural I mean beyond that skin...of eros    and rebuke,    mirror
*Thebes* in Athens, Corinth in *Christ*, *Amerika*

—*the nowhere city,*    *'tis of thee*

seven murals one
seven murals two
seven murals three
seven murals four
**seven murals five**
seven murals six
seven murals seven

An ephemeral archive
of resistance: the momentary vogue
for anti-facial recognition

make-up, before the machines
defeated that intervention—the patterns,
nomadic, becoming a code,

a language of redacted anti-
faces, a residual language
in which for a summer, a fall

we could mark HIC SUNT LEONES,
here is the ghost-site, here
another work of evidentiary

realism, we could mark R U N    R U N
all the swarming decibels
and Simon's intention to witness

into memory, into the ephemeral
gestures of solidarity,
an archive of instants

and traces "you were always you
~~even~~ especially in disguise"
old passport photos, the engines

for generating all the cover profiles,
the mural an homage to that chorus
of disappearing l i g h t e s t   t o u c h

over the surface of your face—*indigo-*
*skinned, white-leopard, mirror-bronze*—
and suddenly g l a s s g l a s s the feeling of it,

all thru the flashback s h a t t e r i n g
of you in the—*blue-lit*—"cinema-room,"
then the stand at FINESTERRE

saturated video of the memory
circulating like a talisman
among the cell & dissidents

under the metastasis sun—*gold, red,*
*red*—clear, violent—*mirror-bronze*—
finding its victims everywhere

## *gate*

A destroyed work. And before. A series of intricate spaces & folds. A destroyed system, destroyed network. And then the sun disappeared. Eclipsed. Blacked-out behind the totality of will. Or you were disappeared from the sun—*gold, red, chromium, bronze, bronze, weapon-grade chrome*—"rain (nuclear)." Weeds. And strange grasses. And other traces of long aftermath. "______ will be abolished when we are abolished." In the epic. And somehow you knew that was code for utopia. The days, countless, and invisible. Redflaresmoke. All thru the sentence. All thru "The Annals," which are themselves destroyed works. Under a redacted sky. "I lost you there in the crush, and thought [red] no [flare] no [smoke] no—" And then the destroying work.—all thru the flashback—searching for you. In the epic—*blue, blue, white-leopard, red.*

*p a s s a g e s*

When I say mural, I mean scripts for the future, scripts for performance, for the open, intervening moment, that transparency—

When I say mural, I mean the architectures of its happening,     the still escape into open seeing  (o r   s a y   t o u c h i n g   h a n d s   t o o)

—*struck-out from the security-state*
*its  d a y   c l e a r  as bombings*—

seven murals one
seven murals two
seven murals three
seven murals four
seven murals five
**seven murals six**
seven murals seven

Grayscale or washed-out, a wall of numbers, / weathered palimpsest, posters, the layers, ongoing / keeping a kind of (real) time, you're in it now, / supersaturated, enfolded, baroque / with the hunt by algorithm, and state-power, / a wall of code, invisible, and then total / *al-Mithar*, the swift & lethal impunity / of those first, terrible weeks in the long century / of dirt, this street, this address, site-specific / memorial, and insurrectionary / form "now desolate / in its silence," *white*, *white-water*, *ash-streaked*, / *white* [phosphorous], *weapon-grade chrome, white-leopard*, / of the security initiative, / Rome creates a desert [in you] and calls it pax / Rome creates a prison in you and calls it Rome, / a sentence, which is really a ban on feeling / the drone & durée——*mirror bronze*—as anything / other than wartime "after the dousing / they didn't let me wash for days, so the chemicals / just kept burning my skin, my eyes," she wrote / "you know we're test-subjects in here, human experiments, / segregated in a place that is no-place," / that security firms perfect chemical / weapons on prisoners was known, was axiom— / *gold, red, chromium*——that lachrymators are thought, / the leading form of thought, (particulate solid) / in the capitaloscence, cut to the thrashes / in the documentary: the animal / thrashes, thrashes (it is on you)—thrashes for a moment then slaughter, / at the 33:00 minute-mark and the voiceover saying: ____________ ______________________________________, then the lion on the reconstructed video, / *al-Namrā'*, the Leopardine, the sound of it over / a glimpse of her hair, running propaganda, wind, desert, / scarf then—*gold, red, chromium, weapon grade chrome*——(on you still)—

# *gate*

Underneath. Never this far below—*redquartz, background dark, red, red, bronze, dirt-black*— Underneath:          and you haven't been here before, this deep in the earth, Iphigenia, you're the second start to the war, and you thought to escape thru the underground—the tunnels—*red, red, bronze, dirt-black*——but they require a description of praxis for entry, and you could only remember t h e beach—redcurrant-colored, remember wanting to take cover, little asylum, but the beach, the open beach, livid with what is h a p p e n i n g— The Radiant, the second start to the war, livid with emergency powers, the sun like kinship—*gold, red, chromium*—bearing down. And underneath The Calamity without relent, halt, break or stay, and you thought to escape, "is it not lawful for all prisoners"——

*passages*

When I say mural I mean when the final treaty of the person, that intricate mask you wear, is love, proximate and remote at once, under sway of a kind of mutuality between the lone and multiple, and the resulting burden

*—to bring it into being*

seven murals one
seven murals two
seven murals three
seven murals four
seven murals five
**seven murals six**
seven murals seven

"they were some of the worst weeks of the century" / "radio active," "radio [or the like] active," / listening to what the series of operations / were like—*black, red, gold, bronze, silver-black, blue, blue, blue*— / listening in absentia, nothing is "like," / everything flows u n d e r n e a t h the colorless, / odorless, and poisonous atmosphere / of the security state, brute combine, / Rauschenbergian chimera—*gold, red, mirror-bronze, / black*—include, the communique / says, "the leading form" of attack, / it changes each time the mural appears, / "which in itself express the ban," the picture displays it— / time, weaponized—abstractly, here it sprawls / over the abandoned industrial park, / (passwords hidden throughout, safe houses, safe-roads) / each building become one of the summer's martyrs, / abstractly—*dancing, they were dancing*—a chorus, / "perilous night," the communique says / "everywhere apparent," / livestreaming from the square, the night after, / and the square intense with keening for the dancers / —*aiai aiai aiai*—the keening, a kind of listening, / imperiled, eliding into waves—*gold, / red, mirror-bronze*— "is it just going to be like this," / constellation, affect, and the *concussive situation, /* as she called it, in the pamphlet from exile, / or prison—the dating of document / is difficult to trace— in exile / listening to the sounds from the cinema-room— / *blue, blue, blue, red, mirror-black*— the leading form of attack, / listening everyday, mediating / on the cells, the prisoners' hunger-strike, / "what would be possible," she wrote "if listening / were the leading-form of being" / include that treatise on openness, include / how force drifts, monstrous Sphinx—*red, gold, chromium*— / with a classical trace, (tho the text is no longer extant) / "Eteolces, you must reckon what is not / possible, what the war forecloses, ceaselessly— / we could live otherwise, you must count the loss / of this counter-life, in your aftermath, / we could be there now, new — *sun-lit dust, / poppy-dotted, glittering*—commons...." / include that utopia, swarming all through / to the end of the value-form, / the day clear—I mean sudden—in its bombings / include "when the open may still escape," / you, the open, sudden—*perfect secrecy*— / in your listening now—

# Ab lish

"The obliteration of the contents of consciousness, the elimination of world ground, which is a condition brought about by the pain and therefore one that once objectified (as it is in confession) should act as a sing of the pain, a call for help, an announcement of a radical occasion for attention and assistance, instead acts to discredit the pain, to render it ... ensure that the pain will be seen and unattended to.

That not only the torturers but the world at large should tend to identify the confession as a "betrayal" makes very overt the fact of his absence of world earns the person in pain not compassion but contempt.

This phenomenon in which the claims of pain are eclipsed by the very loss of world it has brought about is a crucial step in the process of perception that allows one person's physical pain to be understood as another person's power.

"April now, and what does that mean—new earth, it's all, and nothing of

## 12. Mock Burial

And then almost at will the sun disappeared
then almost at will the sun disappeared
almost at will the sun disappeared
at will the sun disappeared
will the sun disappeared
the sun disappeared
sun disappeared
disappeared
appeared
pear
red
ear

disappeared thru the will the sea the annul
then the sun all will stilled disappeared
pain the aleph wielded as star as pain
under willed pain he disappeared
almost red almost ashed pear
as a deer will almost near
devasted in still in pain
dead under the mare
white appears red
heard the rape
bruised red
red tear

## In The Epic

Of these persons, cities, and countries some will need the reckoning of the document, of evidence; some (ruined) will
your sister city; some will disappear under grass and deer; others into the oversound of mourning vowels, bare life loud

include a new era of urban war / include the disappearance of the category 'civilian' / their dying physicalities / how the

In the force-fields of the epic, identity requires the continual extinction of privacy—that obsolete rose—of life not pul
to violence; therefore, you are your geolocation, your SIM card, any and all digital trace, you're nothing less, and nothi

From Nevada, and across those seven thousand infrared miles, you watch—you're the drone's Sensor—
as the blasted man's heat signature, his blood, cools into the gray-black earth, the monochrome of the epic.

include 'alleged combatants' / include their transformations / says the essay from 1940 / include "the blind cause of dis
the arrow that flieth          by that intelligence

¡sicarios se arrepientan! read the signs of the teenagers in metallic face-paint, robes, and dingy angel-wings who stand
in the siren lights of murder sites, at intersections, at crossroads throughout Ciudad Juárez, this weird street-theatre th

The street as public sphere clamoring with opinion; the street as a space of circulation and exchange; as in the phrase
the street as dance floor, that first theatre and station of the defeated; on this Oakland corner, the dancers' bodies—th

include the "small fragments of war enshrined in ordinary life" / include ordinary life as small fragments inside the tot

If you bring forth what is within you—your beautiful death—what you bring forth will save you: the future ghost of yo
If you do not bring forth your beautiful death, your beautiful death will destroy you, which is the gospel of the epic.

"They've no more disease in the heart / because they love to die / haya! / hayaalal jihad!" triumphs the video: clips of se
streaming on the vibe and technics of a violent chic, and the fuck of it all is, Achilles would recognize their jihad—its s

already in the first year the civil war had made its mark / a new candor had entered into the lanaguage / sick of orname

She had a city: she had a city of final treaties, a city divided; in a thieves' cant city, she sped, practically a centaur on he
she made a city of exhausted tenderness, a city spoken out of powerlessness; she had a city, then the sea rose; before th

In the fable there is no war, so it had to be invented: you loved contests, so a contest was called, and later at the Festiv
from your thousand-eyed throne—how could you not—you were emperor of all these marvels arrayed before you, and

of force multipliers / include the colorless, odorless, and weaponized epic of unit 450 / include the geometry of targeti
a ragged and wordless music / include

The grotesque horseplay; the frenzied screamer; the fat one with a desperate look; the fetal; and maybe a survivor, his
burnt, his skull open: the whole traumatized crater of them in Jeff Wall's *Dead Troops Talk (A Vision after an Ambush of a*

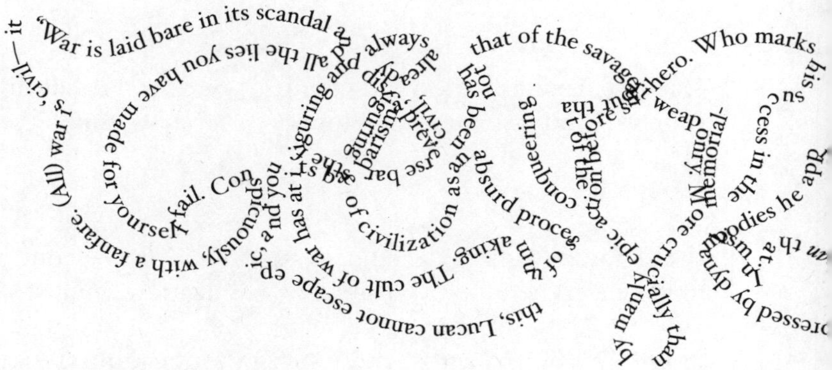


rackle along the clouted grain of lo-fi—Radio Free Disaster,
with them—and could that keening yet rupture the epic?

become proof—no longer persons—of the epic

licly open
g more than metadata in the superinformation epic.

ster," / the arrow that flieth by day by night / by nightvision, include the protocols of a signature strike, //

or hours (sometimes on stilts or chairs)
eir only weapon in the epic.

the Arab street," the street is the popular mind, the polis proper; the street, imperial, where all roads lead to Rome, to riots;
articulate grace the body is hieroglyphic, machine-like, balletic—become an elegy for those unremembered by the epic.

-war century's epic / of biopolitics / of necropolitcs / of a fire that never sinks nor sets / include that riddle too

reaching out to meet your living hand....

ered rivers, severed cities, severed persons,
ng-drenched propaganda—as the epic.

t and classicism, / she set out into the vernacular / of now describe this / include her odyssey / the anti-epic you're trying for

bike; already in the first verse she had a city destroyed; back in the twentieth century she made a city from blessed straining;
sea rose, she had a City of Otherwise & If (friends' eyes were polis)—can this be true again, or ever was—nowhere in the epic.

of Mirror Blossom Lake, as the country's wizards, doctors, artists, scientists, sorcerers, and prophets all presented their spells a
aw at once that no one amazement could equal the idea of war, but rather, war must graph the totality of it all—an eclipse. And

solutions / and the will by which those arrows fly / include the red team analysis / their skepticism, a minor halt only / include a

hock-intense gaze; the tough calm of the cliché sergeant; those dead (not otherwise characterized); that lost, stoned-on-eternity
*ed Army Patrol, near Moqor, Afghanistan, Winter 1986)* is like Lucan's Latin grammar in *Civil War,* but will epic warring on the epic ev

of the First and Second Worlds cannot but confl…
you not 'Post-War' heritage, feel your collusion
still reading Lucan's poem, you …
in the …nd desires … conflict. You
have for comprehending historical reality."
media you
impossible sea
charisma of 'heroism' on the part of the
complicity in the … cannot escape
O sing, System, of the fin… treato to the person, that coast of
This isn't what narrative you
can narrate
you have no way to tell the story.
differences constructed and confirmed by war have shrunk towards zero, when there is only one side…
When victim is victor, when the

…gainst Envisioning: *For a year or more I've been suspended in the desire to write* …*tter—a letter against envisioning. A letter to rhyme with* soliel cou coupé. *A letter* …*ent, and not its history, a letter contra document, the living word, I yet try to believe* …*ere already my thinking gets caught up in some imaginary, already I'm drifting into* …*ng, its empty key. Graffiti has always been my escape route out of this bind, since there* …*nd the city are one, yet increasingly I sense its limitations, not its possibilities. A* …*y world, other than this one, forever seems the coast of Bohemia, and the voyage* …*the most improbable sea. I know you're committed to the imagination as a force for,* …*ience of liberty—a leading towards that human world. "We never could have ended* …*ation and apartheid without the imagination, nor could the prisoners have suvived* …*aving had access to a real counter-force to their imprisonment. The imagination* …*jailed hour, each jailed minute also a possible opening into the freedoms of thought,* …*ent, and endurance. It is also through the imagination that I reckoned my crime of* …*nd even after joining the struggle that there was a real crime to confess." I was high* …*ought, and vision the first time I read these sentences of yours, I felt myself in the* …*ready for the setting out, and you there, across the river looking straight at me. And I* …*ver gainsay your experience and history, but I'm lost to the imagination now. "Work* …*of work," Cecila says as I'm leaving after having read to her that day, and I know* …*it artistically, that working will lead to more work, keep melancholy and depression* …*I've come to hear it as a spell against the imagination, against envisioning: if we're* …*to that universal beach, it will be made, it will be terraformed—and by force. I'm* …*the park, and a storm has come.     More soon.     Love     J.*

…s, their engines, works, and machines, you swooned
in the mind, indestructible, ceaseless, is the verse you added to the epic.

…sura, / a turn to whitespace, then //

…he one soldier; another blasted,
…lize the epic?

# Force Drift

*—one of the chorus, whispers / to you a sentence of perfect / secrecy*], in a long century / of dirt, seabeast,songbird, green-breasted / orator, greenest that first greenness / after—*black [sunlight], silver-gray [air], weapon-grade chrome*— / fire-bombs, then rain, seabird, beastsong, / "we reject cruelty," out under / or through the insurrection / in a long century of dirt / "touch, too, is an infinite system / of communication," she wrote me / from the restoration of the senses, / and that thought in which mutuality / is sheltering against the long / century of dirt, she wrote me: / "I am only ever trying to trace / that sense—fugitive, glassy, a kind of surface / tension—of the beautiful reciprocity / in the secrecy of correspondence," / I kept that letter through the total- war / sentence, and her missing [ ], the thinking / lost therein—*gold, silver, / red, indigo-skinned*—a river / (a printer's error, sure, / but could be elegy or cryptography, / pink teeth, a book code) in the small arms survey, / a wine-dark-wave, / "privacy, quickening" / invisible, and yet all fields are allusive / "is it just going be be like this" / graffitied all over the city / tire-smoke, elsewhere, she wrote me: / "which in itself expresses the ban," / I tried to burn the grief, / thought of it as a letter in betrayal, / and tried to burn it among Salp'uri / swaths, the rite didn't take / erasure, in the Athenian case, / meant banning memory, meant painting / the lines out—writing *law* over / the whiteout surface, / the long century of it, / in the blue notebook, she wrote: "I come from a country / where the bodies were not given back, what future," pink teeth, *indigo-skinned*—

# Force Drift

pink teeth, *indigo-skinned*—the rite didn't avail / which in itself express the ban / she wrote: "I come from a country where the bodies / were not given back, what future—" / is it just going to be this— / *the grass still wet with it all* / in the epic, rage (mēnis)—*gold, red, chromium,* / *bronze, mirror-bronze*—is the ordeal (fire) through which / you break into the real(m) of perception, / gate & passage into sensibility itself / through the violent (beautiful) annihilation / [that consumes] of the same capacity / in others—*gold, red, red* [paint-stick oil-crayons]— / [they pour along] a few regard the messenger's speech, / at a loss (and the story a fire / [that forces all before it] that forces itself / through your L V N G person) for the *Fifty* / *Days at* ______ (all destroyed cities in those missing syllables) / [and graphite] exhausted from the chase—*the grass still* / *red with it all*—at a loss at how the messenger's speech, / [sweeps the whole earth into a fire of L V N G / syllables] a litany of warcrimes (and even / there story wraps itself around the casualties / hissing, now calling itself *reparative justice*) / could vanish by being spoken aloud, / "the rites almost never take," she wrote "and yet and yet" / the grass a counter-message scratched out, asemically / [in oil-crayons and graphite]—like a force that consumes / everything, Father Saffron a "permanent war-camp" / he also disappeared a city into sea / I heard you say in book code, / I heard you say through the palimpsest grasses, / —*still red with it all*—say goodbye to red August, Catullus, / say goodbye to the fourteen strophes, to the twelve techniques / to that which forces all before into the sea, / the sea that burning that is fire / say goodbye to that beach (do you remember) / in Asia Minor under a metastasis sun— / *gold, red, chromium, weapon-grade bronze*—"the city / is strictly performative," she wrote me: / "you take an oath—*mirror-bronze*— / "I shall not recall the misfortunes."

# In The Epic

To The Lord Protector, to the Supreme Commander Allied Forces, to Dear Leader, Lode Star of the Twenty-First C
Father of Devastations, to the All-Crushing Centcom, to the Perfect Picture in whom Tears Disappear, to Mother C

"Where am I—what is this place?" // "I'm sorry. I know you've never been so deep in the earth before—his police w

I want to re-invent language to make a new hieroglyph in which the social and psychic intermingle to confront polit
a hieroglyph yet to be anarchic to reject masculine hero-worship to disperse images texts silences I typed these rep

"You see it everywhere from then—in Guillermo's *drugwar*, in Lucy's *Trilogy*, and Susan's *Kalash* portraits, and all of
a time came when none of us could use the figure without it standing on the violent ground of the epic."

"I think I remember the war. I remember—before the war—the beach: redcurrant-colored, pomegranate—the

Everything flows: as in the analysis of a complex system or network, those glowing thickets mapping how capital m
the connections and viral spread of reportage—and the actions that set it off—and you were there in the real-time c

And then, suddenly, you will be the city, and the city—for want of being any other (ecstatic) body—will be an insurr
of verse." And the city that had been (riven, panoptic, oligarchic, and false treaty of the person) will swarm out into

"Like you yourself are the messenger disappearing at the end of the road, no, some feeling—*I think I remember*—
before the war, before the redflare smoke filling the city, before the white phosphorous sun (do you understa

Seabeast, songbird, green-breasted orator, / greenest the first greenness after // firing-lines then rain, fire-bombs the
the riot police, the graffiti wheeling under moonlight and adrenaline, // spinning (Blake's eyes) / that fiery collective

Through the dream's diffusion-filtered light you feel the wear of time, oceanic, between them: the dissident-in-exile
and you're the diligent investigator on the trail of the Secretary of Atrocities, lost in the archive, lost in "the desire c

"I remember their approach, the armies, everyone watching from the rooftops, waiting, the gates like movie screens

The remains are received clad in a white shirt, and white pajama-type pants; feces covers the body and clothes belo
of the mid-back, and satellite contusions, massive internal hemorrhages. But the fighting (that lead to the capture t

The battle for Los Angeles; the battle for São Paulo; the battles of Cairo and Caracas; the sieges of Astana, and East
the attack on Paris mirroring the attack on Beirut, the falls of Damascus, of Lagos, of Kabul, and Mexico City; by t

"I think I remember the aftermath, I remember the widows, keening from the rooftops, redcurrant-colored, *aiai*

After the long total-war century; after indefinite detention; after the state of exception, after its myriad renditions,
which revolves forever around the RADIANT POINT!" After the constellations—every idea is a sun, every sun a star, a r

“My fear is that the indefinite detainment of prisoners on Guantanamo, for whom no rights of appeal will be possible within
el for federal courts, will be no rights of appearing … ouge
some … governing sites … who may be treated … international … ition … recogn … ibute rights of recogn

ntury, to the Master of the Computer that Surveils the World, to Father Saffron,
›urage, admit these songs (for survival's polity) epilogue-like, our fucking anti-epic.

re coming, I didn't have a choice, I had to bury you here.”

cal obscenities I drew the articulate grace the body is
ts a paper mural to unmake the epic.

Vei Tran's photographs—and beyond any kind of history painting;

minutes billowing like redflare smoke—then some rougher color (was father always angry), then the beach is gone or I am.” //

ves, or the animated graphics depicting the process, not static fact, each indifferent cloud is, as in the lines tracking
it, too, safe at your screen: “IRG's helicopter's flying low, right now creating a devastating sound,” disaster sounds unto the ep

:tionary wave, a carrier-wave, a wave of living perception...“we live by the urgent / wave
he human, finally—and the city that was yet to come, the ideal of it, ~~a struck-through epic~~.

returns, then ebbs, and each wave of—*I think I remember*—the redcurrant-colored beach carries the feeling further away
d ), and each return is more real, less living. And something else: already I feel part of an Ever.”

rain. / Seabird, beastsong out over, or through ruin: // *we reject humiliation* in spray-painted / Arabic, spinning as we try to outr
of letters, of lives we abandoned, // so we chose, against our better / universalism, the meanest orator, immortal epic.

her dancer daughter, as you pace their separate thoughts, long commutes, disappearances, the video-call lost to buffering....Ar
lled utopia,” | then the Lion of Lions, Whose Voice Is Loudest With History, assumes—brazen aristeia—this mass grave and r

under the glowing marty-prosters—blazoned like shields. I think I remember, or did I read this in a book, was this somec

the waist; there is a confluence of red-purple-black contusions surrounding the torso between the breasts and coastal margin;
at lead to the torture that lead to the homicide that lead to this autopsy report) shines sublime—and that's the glamour of the

erusalem; the battle for Islamabad; the stand at Mumbai; the stand at Mosul (then its fall); the stand at Kobanê; the battles fc
e time you read this, o men of Athens in your new Age of Reason (being at best a no-fly zone), the battles of Jakarta, Kiev, and

*iai aiai* I remember the messanger come to collect me, a trophy, slave or one last killing on the beach—this time a boy tc

edactions, and obliterations; after the researches, the reports, and excavations; after another (final) treaty of the person—“tha
dical halt and rupture, now—after all the other reckonings, what is the poem, Jeff, | some kind of Caliban left to curse the lang

ement this ext... takes place, we will see the resurgence of lawless and illegitimate power ... a violent ... self-aggrandizing state sovereignty at the expense of any commitment that might support global cooperation ... to govern according to standards that ought ... if not, for the time being, ... the treatment of humans. We have yet to become human, it seems, and that prospect seems even more radically ... at the water front,

"If I could sketch the future / of persons I'd make a fire / bombed street, then its first greenness." Do you believe that we are forever changed ... the time being indefinitely foreclosed." for, if not, imperiled, who die in front of ... I stand // the "will bring a widow's grief / now as their paraphernalia / to second marriages. It blunts mind. Hell is a song in terza rima / washed rifles." the sky the sheen of oil / defeated. // Wives "Virgil blesses / those who die before their fathers' eyes // those who die before their homes / in their city's alleys // those who die defending / resisting who lie / nonetheless of their wives, those who die /

*include The Calamity, Whose Voice Is Loudest / include the oversound / The Overwhelm, The Cause For Wild Assertions / include The Wolf, / Who Accumulates, Who Multiplies Until All Else Is Eclipsed / include the totality / of their dying physicalities / include Father Saffron, Who Destroys Capital / The Indomitable, Whose Coat Is Red, Who Eats Until He Chokes (also said of the epic) / include The Radiant, The Sublime (also said of The Seer, The Guide) / include the halt and rupture / of their dying physicalities / and history loud with them / include Cassandra / the idea of Cassandra / of speech, prophetic / albeit unheeded / unacknowledged / like the lyric / you were about to say / like the anti-epic you're trying for / the counter-dream, the dream to end the epic / include her graffiti-book, the book of when writing, image, and the city are one, The Book of Walls / include The City of Otherwise & If / which could exist / which could exist as beastsong and redcurrant dawn exists / in the eyes of freinds / o fiery collective which could exist / as insurrections / as hunger strikes, drone strikes, devastations, and ruins exist / include the redflare smoke over the city / then its first greenness as immortal epic exists*

it like?"

t's 2054
; epic.

; life?"

barring

nkers' cities (Hong Kong, London, New York, Zürich);
will have had become the epic.

te the frame, or I was the messenger bringing the red-colored message.

n
the epic?

# Force Drift

The city is strictly performative: you eat
paper, it's ordeal & passage, a trance—*gold, red,*
*chromium, weapon-grade bronze*—and the abolition

of men, a password you made through obliteration
& performance, a transmission of ardor,
in memory now a reaction: parts per million of you

and "privacy, quickening"—*gold, red, chromium*—
Strange flora wilding the aftermath city,
martyr-crown, I heard you say of or through metastasis,

there in the small arms survey, a book code,
against the terror-logic of reversals & doubles:

FEAR UP HARSH    EGO DOWN    ISOLATION    FUTILITY

bite on that, o men of Athens, the mouth to tear
at swaths,      and carcinogens, it never leaves you
does it, the long sentence of the traumaeffect,

radicalized, transmogrified through the postures—
*weapon-grade bronze*—your body took, oracular
punk, Sibylline in faded black jeans, first poised—

*chromium*—above the bowl of melted snow,
then the soaked swaths, impossible communion,
you gagging, arachnidian, on the vehement sun of it—

*gold, red, fire-black*—ritual against infliction, against
the body turned instrument of infliction—*gold, gold,*
*weapon-grade bronze*—ritual for the body alchemical,     and yet.

into annals of redaction
and obliteration

the sun itself
a ghost detainee

## Force Drift

After. The messenger's speech. The vehement sun of it—
    *gold, red, chromium.* The long century of it. Sentence
of indefinite detention. And how many
    breaths you can absent. Under. The twelfth technique.

The blank. Totality of it. Eclipses. "Simon's
    intention to witness something." She wrote me:
"The formulation of the body as proof returns."
    In this force drift. Of or thru the metastasis

sun—*weapon-grade bronze.* And yet—and yet. Abolish
    something. Starting with the school of americas.
Abolish the fire. That never sets. Nor relents. ABOLISH
    graffitied all over the postwar city.

After Brumaire. She sent the blue notebook. On the cover,
    she wrote: "There is no postwar city."

# A Sun to Summon the Snow

ai

---

This was meant to be an essay, a kind of science against the day—against day + night as nothing more than instruments of human pain, on-going, indefinite measure, the cell, the century of it.

ai

---

This was meant to be part of the conversation we thought we'd have the time for. The hourglass on my desk pacing letters to you—thru it all, and after now.

ai
ai

ai

ai

ai

---

Because it will never arrive, and is therefore useless,
imagine this other version, the impossible object,
the anti-epic we were trying for:

ai

ai

ai ai

ai

ai

---

the film of it (saturated digital
video), a collage of memory,

ai

ai

ai

---

document, and invention riding
the desire for a reckoning tense——

ai

ai ai

ai

ai

ai

ai

ai

---

*irrefutable as the sun to the eye*——

ai
ai ai

ai

ai

ai
ai

ai

ai

ai

ai

---

I had wanted a language, to write a language of the eye
taking in the sun, the black star totality of it—

ai

ai ai

ai
ai

ai

ai

ai

ai ai

ai
ai

---

then the blotched light aftermath of having written the end of the world.

ai

ai

ai

---

Though we never reached that shore—

ai

ai

ai

ai

ai

ai

ai

ai

ai

ai

ai

ai

ai

ai

ai

---

for the waves, the waves—*cobalt, lapis lazuli,*
*high blue,* Prussian—glistening, digital,

ai ai

ai

ai

ai

ai

ai

ai

ai

---

and nowhere close to the real.

ai
ai
ai
ai ai

ai
ai

ai
ai

ai
ai
ai

ai
ai ai

ai
ai

ai

ai

ai
ai
ai

ai

ai
ai

ai
ai

ai
ai
ai

ai

ai ai
ai

ai

ai

ai

ai

ai

ai ai

ai

ai

ai

ai

ai

ai

ai ai

ai

ai

ai

ai

ai ai

ai

ai

ai

ai

ai

ai

ai

ai

ai

ai

ai ai

---

"When I think of anywhere, I'm truly thinking
of a place that cannot (yet) be,"
you wrote in your last letter from exile.

ai
ai

ai

ai

ai

ai

ai

ai

ai

---

This was meant to be a letter from that not-yet-nowhere.

ai

ai ai

ai

ai ai

ai

ai

ai

ai

ai

ai ai

---

A letter from the era of last measures:
the seed-vault opening to arctic air,
survivors setting out in the new weathers,

ai

ai

ai

ai

ai

ai

ai

ai

ai

ai ai

ai

ai

ai

---

the beginning
of an addressable reality,
beyond our time-sensitive skin,

ai

ai ai

ai

ai ai

ai

ai

ai

ai ai

ai

ai

ai

ai

ai

ai

ai

---

the theory of the person [ ] therein.

ai

ai

ai

ai

ai ai

ai

ai ai

ai

ai

ai

ai

ai ai

---

I had wanted to write a language—*to music*
*a language*—*language a music*—equal
to the disaster, the long cell of it—

ai

ai
ai

ai

ai

ai ai

ai

ai

ai

ai

---

the lion mouth of it—*gold, red, chromium, bronze.*

ai

ai

ai

ai

ai

ai

ai

ai

ai "ghost ai

ai "ghost ai

ai

ai

---

Impossible any first syllable—

ai
ai ai
ai
ai
ai
ai
ai
ai
ai
ai
ai
ai
ai
ai
ai ai
ai
ai
ai
ai
ai
ai
ai
ai ai
ai

ai ai
ai
ai

ai

ai
ai
ai
ai

ai

ai
ai

ai
ai

ai

ai

ai
ai

ai ai
ai

ai

ai

ai ai
ai ai
ai

ai ai
ai
ai

ai
ai
ai

ai
ai
ai

ai

ai
ai
ai

ai

ai
ai
ai

ai

ai
ai
ai

ai
ai

ai
ai

ai

ai

ai

ai

---

rather, an installation of that sound [ ]

ai ai
ai

ai

ai

ai

ai

ai

ai

ai
ai

ai

ai

ai

ai

ai

ai

ai

ai

ai

Ai

ai

ai

ai

ai

ai

ai

ai ai

ai

ai

ai

ai

ai ai ai

ai

ai

ai

ai

AI

AI

ai

ai

ai

ai

ai

ai ai

ai

ai

ai

ai

ai
ai

ai
ai

ai
ai

ai

ai ai

ai

ai
ai

ai

ai

ai

ai ai

ai ai

ai ai

ai

ai

ai Ai

ai

ai

ai ai

ai

ai

ai

ai

ai

ai

ai

ai ai

ai

ai

ai

ai

ai

ai

ai

ai

ai

ai
ai

ai

ai
ai
ai

ai
ai

ai

ai

ai
ai
ai
ai

ai
ai

---

the justice [ ] therein—

ai

ai

ai

ai ai

ai

ai

ai

ai

ail

ai

ai

ai ai

ai

ai

ai

ai

ai

ai

ail

ai

ai

ai

ai

ai

ai

ai

ai

ai

ai

ai

ai

ai ai

ai

ai

ai

ai

ai ai

ai

ai

ai

ai

ai

ai ai

ai ai

A I

ai

A I

ai

---

against the—*gold, red, chromium*—century—

ai

ai ai

ai

ai

ai ai

ai

---

*black, black*—cell—*dirt-red, wet-red, fire-red,*

ai

ai

ai

ai

ai

ai

ai

ai

---

*mirror-bronze*—sun.

ai

ai

ai

ai

Ai

ai

# Notes

The writing and research into *Force Drift* began with a problem and question: since there will be no true judicial or political reckoning for the authors and agents of the torture program, can cultural forms such as poetry embody an alternative, albeit lesser, form of accountability? *Force Drift* is motivated by this search for that reckoning tense within poetry answer to this question; further, *Force Drift* is dedicated to the all those who suffered under the vehement sun of American imperial violence, finding its victims everywhere.

The enumeration and litany of colors that appear throughout *Force Drift* are sometimes direct citations and sometimes inspired extensions of the dynamic use of color in *War Music,* Christopher Logue's radical and essential adaptation of the *Illiad.*

*Tazhib* is a calligraphic and illumination tradition and visual vocabulary found within Islamic art particularly in Arabic, Farsi, and Turkic (as wellas other languages); although the practice and aesthetic of t*azhib* can be traced to pre-Islamic Iran, it's decorative, geometric visual vocabulary flourished within the strictures against image-making within Islam. I first encountered *tazhib*in the artwork of Hedieh Javanshir Ilchi, when I was commissioned to write a poem in response to one her paintings ("Too bad, you let me go") in her Traveler series. I was deeply inspired by Ilchi's juxtaposition of *tazhib* within a visual economy that also included perspective and representation of the human figure. I approached my poem in response to the painting less an instance of ekphrasis, but rather, as a translation; and further a translation inspired by Walter Benjamin's idea that through the act of translation the so-called target language can be transformed by the encounter with the source language. My incorporation of the *tazhib* patterns into the poems of *Force Drift* is a result of this double inspiration: the juxtaposition of decorative, non-representational illumination aesthetics and economies of figuration; as well as the ideal that translation can change the language—its expressive capacity—through the encounter with, openness to, and respect for difference. Across *Force Drift*, the *tazhib* patterns perform different functions; sometimes the *tazhib* act as illumination (to the poem or archival document) acting as a paratext bearing language almost as an epigraph albeit one that moves in and out of legibility as the language flows along the vectors of arabesques, other times the *tazbib* becomes the body text of a visual poem.

Of the genre of the "corpse poem," Diana Fuss writes: "the speaking corpse operates as a figure for poetry itself, a dead voice that refuses to remain silent, a spectral genre that continues to speak and walk abroad," and this spectral persistence struck me as especially cogent to the question of how cultural forms like poetry or history might serves alternative albeit lesser forms of reckoning for the war crimes of America in the so-called global war on terror.

The design of "Mural" is loosely based on the play *Seven Against Thebes*; however, rather than an ekphrasis of the advancing general's shield which structures Aeschylus's play, my sequence of gate, passages, mural culminates with the ekphrasis of an imaginary mural. John Tipton's engagements and adaptation of Seven Against Thebes and Ajax have both been inspirations for my own work in relation to Greek tragedy, which as a discourse holds within in it a critique of the epic: in tragedy the hero is the problem.

# Index

## Acknowledgments

Sincere and abiding gratitude to the editors of the following journals in which versions of the poems from *Force Drift* first appeared: of these poems have appeared in Academy of American Poets Poem-a-Day; Writing Utopia (UK); Best American Experimental Writing 2015 (digital), and Best American Experimental Writing 2020 (print); Bat City Review; Colorado Review; Denver Quarterly; Seattle Review; Swamp Pink; Tupelo Quarterly; and The Best of Tupelo Quarterly; White Wall Review (CA); Neck; VOLT; diSonare (CDMX); and Manifold Criticism.

Additionally, I've understand performance to be an important heuristic into the refinement and revision of this *essay in the epic*, I want to thank the curators who have opened space for me to explore the work of *Force Drif*t in significant performance: The Poetry Project at St Marks (2014 & 2019); Enclave Poéticas Rituales (Mexico City); and most crucially at the Summer Writing Program at Naropa University, which I've directed with Anne Waldman since 2016.

Thanks to the editors at Tupelo Press for their commitment to and care for my work, especially Kristina Marie Darling whose long care and advocacy for my work over the years has been so very heartening.

I am grateful to Naropa University for the support of the publication of this book, and for providing me an intellectual, imaginative zone out of which to write this last decade.

To my friends and fellow writers—too many to name here—whose visionary company both on the page, and in real rooms and hours has sponsored, influenced, inspired, complicated, contradicted, or otherwise inflected the shape of these poems, thank you—

Special thanks to Dan Beachy-Quick for being an ardent friend to this book along its path of appearance. And to Matthew Moore for being a reader of epic incursion.

Love and gratitude to Patrick Pethybridge (whose near whole life has been paralleled by the making of this book) for your deep compassion and equanimity, and for the sage reminder to let go of fear, and occupy oneself with creative work.

Gratitude and love beyond all measure to Carolina Ebeid—so sweet is thy discourse to me, that if these pages sing beyond the catastrophe they reckon, that singing is a devotion to you.

All remaining thanks.